# WISH ME LUCK AS YOU WAVE ME GOODBYE

A Selection of Northumbrian Memories of World War 11

by  Jane  Torday

W0008513

The Spredden Press, Brocksbushes Farm, Stocksfield,
Northumberland NE45 7WB. Telephone 043471 3100/3400
Fax 043471 2965.

Printed by the Tyneside Free Press, Charlotte Square, Newcastle
on Tyne.


ISBN   1 871739 06 3

"All the business of war, and indeed
all the business of life, is to
endeavour to find out what you don't
know by what you do."

                    The Duke of Wellington.

To my Father and my Uncle

# CONTENTS

## ACKNOWLEDGEMENTS

There are many people I would like to thank for their kindness and their help, in so many different ways, while I was writing this book. For fear of leaving one out, I have decided not to name my friends, but they all know who they are. I would, however, like to say a special thank-you to my husband and my sons for their tolerance towards the obsession of someone trying to get a book out on time and not infrequently word-processing their way through lunch and supper.

In direct connection with the book, I must say a particularly heartfelt thankyou to Bill Purdue, who carved out chunks of time from his own very busy agenda to function as my editor. He also wrote the Preface, and we worked together on the introductions to each contributor. He was always ready to discuss and inform, and if his patience and good humour were put to the test sometimes, he never showed it. I would like to thank Pete Swann from the Tyneside Free Press for preparing the book for print and for his sympathetic approach to the job. I would like to thank Gillian Dickinson for her enthusiasm and for including me in her Spreddon Press list of Northumbrian books. I would like to thank Julia Harrison for rescuing me with her superior knowledge of computers, when my new word processor and I were on the verge of a form of contemporary warfare, woman versus machine. In addition, I would beg the tolerance of my readers, should they stumble accross any misspelt word which may yet be lurking in some paragraph, despite assiduous checking before going to print.

Most important of all, I would like to thank all of those kind people who gave me of their time and of themselves to contribute their wartime stories. Finally, I would like to raise a cheer for The Soldiers' Sailors' and Airman's Families Association who provided me with some of my finest contributors. Thank you all.

PREFACE.

The fiftieth anniversary of the outbreak of the Second World War is, inevitably, bitter-sweet for those who lived through that war. Memories recollect comradeship, achievements and the tortuous path to final victory, but also, danger and the deaths of friends and relations. How long ago it all seems and how different, that world of uniforms, ration cards and steam trains; yet how close and reclaimable it can also seem, for this was the world of youth or childhood.

Oral history gives us accounts of individual war-time experiences which would not otherwise be retrievable. Inevitable limitations are that much time has elapsed between experience and the recollection, while so much has been written about the war and so many T.V. programmes and films made, that memory has to go through a prism of imposed images and opinions. The man or woman of seventy confronts a younger self of twenty and tries to remember what that younger self felt; to what extent does the older, and perhaps wiser, self modify or even unwittingly censor the emotions of the younger? But these accounts that Jane Torday has brought together are vivid and unpretentious and defy such cautions.

If the experience of war is one common denominator of these accounts, the background of Northumberland is the other.Why Northumberland? Why a collection of county memories? Surely Britain mobilised for war at the direction of central governement and the country, not the county, went to war. Yet the nation is the sum of its parts and it is from our "little platoons" that we reach out to the wider national identity. In 1939 counties were much more important social and cultural units than, alas, they are now, when some historic counties have disappeared from the map and others, like Northumberland, suffered severe surgery with the insensitive reorganisation of local government. The old Northumberland had a real identity based on shared traditions and affirmed by a less mobile and more homogeneous population than we have today.

Some fought their wars within the R.A.F., or in new elite units like the Paratroop Regiment, and in other army units without Northumbrian connections; while the sea-faring tradition of the county ensured a substantial contribution of officers and men to the Royal Navy and the Merchant Marine. However, many in the army fought as Northumbrians in regiments which drew upon the county, as did the contributors to this book who served with the Royal Northumberland Fusiliers and the Northumberland Hussars.

This book does not pretend to present proportional cross sections of either social categories or the different war-time services and occupations. Here are simply seventeen accounts by seventeen interesting men and women: their histories and their wars. They encompass men and women combatants and civilians, officers and other ranks, countrymen and urban workers, an army chaplain, and a small boy growing up in wartime.

These accounts do not, of course, constitute a history of the war, though Captain Baker- Cresswell's story and that of Wing Commander Kayll do cast new light on such diverse matters as the cracking of the Enigma Code and the "Wooden Horse" escape. It is interesting and revealing how many campaigns, battles and major features of the war were encountered in seventeen individual histories: the Norwegian campaign, Dunkirk, the Battle of Britain, the Battle of the Atlantic, Greece, Crete, the sinking of the Bismarck, the Fall of Singapore,the Normandy landings, Arnhem, the Burma campaign, the surrender of the German Forces in the North West and the liberation of Hong Kong. The world of POW camps in Germany is described by three raconteurs and the horror of the Burma railway by another.

Wars are essentially fought by a generation - "People" were, after all,"young then", as William Benson puts it. "People" are one's own generation; one's parents and their contemporaries or one's children and their's are not in the same sense "People". The Generals and Admirals may have been older, the Home Guard have done their bit and`older workers and managers kept factories going, while war-time children endured evacuation and some modest hardship. But the war was waged by those twixt eighteen and their early forties, and those who were in it from the beginning are septuagenarians at the least, now. We can only be grateful that they rose to the challenge so well, and marvel at the good humour and even affection with which, as these histories show, they still regard their personal wars.

William Purdue.

# INTRODUCTION

Some twenty seven years ago, I sat on Utah Beach in Normandy, eating a picnic with my father. My mother and younger brother and sister had disappeared into the distance to gather shells and build sandcastles. It was as peaceful a family scene as one could wish for, on a sandy beach on a summer's day.

Yet the beach, Utah beach, had in its time been witness to a very different kind of scene. In June 1944, Utah Beach had been host to infantry divisions of the US First Army when they landed to play their part on D Day in operation 'Overlord', the Allied Invasion into occupied Europe, the largest military operation undertaken in our history.

Iain Macleod, who was attached to the 50th Northumbrian Division on D Day described his feelings when he awoke, on his ship in the channel, that day, and saw this great Armada all about him."As full light began to come, one saw the ships and planes. It was a sight so paralysing that tears came to my eyes. It was as if every ship that had ever been launched was there, and even as if the sea had yielded up her wrecks. It was as if every plane that had ever been built was there, and so, it seemed in fantasy, as if the dead crews were there too. There had never been since time began such a rendezvous for fighting men: there never will be again." (Spectator, 1964.)

My father explained something of this to his thirteen year old daughter as he munched his way thoughtully through his French bread and Camembert. I cannot describe it now, as he did then, but I can remember quite clearly, experiencing a strong sense of history, of almost touching history, as I sat on Utah beach that afternoon. I also appreciated for the first time, that World War 11, which was history to me, had infact been a reality for my father.

I was so interested by what I was hearing, that I was determined to keep this conversation going as long as possible. My father, for his part, warmed to his theme, pleased that he had lit a spark in the daughter who usually grumped whenever we stopped to visit one of the numerous military graveyards which chequer Northern France; an activity which I always felt took up valuable time on our French holidays.

I had known that my father had been a prisoner of war, but I knew nothing of any action he had fought prior to that, or where he had been prisoner for how long, or what he had felt about it. So I did not quite ask, "What did you do in the war, Daddy?" But I did say, "When were you taken prisoner?"

My father answered this question and many more. What he revealed was , for me, the beginning of an interest, not so much in war itself, but in how people survive extremely testing circumstances and of the extraordinary qualities of courage, of comradeship, of humour, which stress can bring out in human beings.

 As the tide came in and the afternoon shadows started to lengthen, he unfolded the story of his war to me. He told me of his capture in Belgium, fighting an action on the Louvain canal in May 1940 and of the subsequent five years in different German and Polish prison camps. As I listened to him, I became increasingly aware of how extraordinary it was that my father, a man who went to work, had dinner parties, made jokes, relaxed in his garden, took his family on holiday, led a completely normal life, should have lived through all this too. After all, I was young enough for a five year stint in prison to seem more like twenty years.

But there it was. He told me his story, and I have always remembered that afternoon together. It made a deep impression on me and it produced a feeling of particular sympathy and respect not only for my father, but for my parents' and grandparents' generation, for those who had lived through one if not two wars.

This September 1989, we commemorate the anniversary of our declaration of war on Germany in 1939. Fifty years have passed, half a century, and many of those who played their part in the last war are in the autumn, if not the winter, of their years. Volumes on the subject of the last war already exist, and many more are being published this year. It suddenly occurred to me that this might be a moment to add one more publication to this list. I thought that it might provide a small, but interesting addition to the records, if I were to talk to people in the county where I now live, Northumberland, about their wartime experiences.

Northumbrians enjoy a certain reputation for being good soldiers and for being sound people. Talking to a number of them over the past few months has confirmed that reputation , to me, as being entirely justified.

I have also been immensely touched by the degree of kindness, and co-operation which I encountered when I approached people - people who after all, had no reason to invite me into their homes and give me their views on things.

After explaining the intentions of my book to them, their reaction was very often, "I'll do anything I can to help."
I also discovered in the main, that people were very modest about their own part in things. It has to be said that some were so modest, that they felt that it would be inappropriate to include them in the book. Very often their accounts were both entertaining and illuminating but they felt that they would not stand up to scrutiny on the printed page.

Courage takes many forms, and one of those is undoubtedly humour.Some of the darkest hours of those I talked too, were suddenly and unexpectedly illuminated by anecdotes that were hilarious, absurd, or demonstrated the resourcefulness and innovation that people are capable of in truly awful moments.

Each account is different, as one would expect it might be. These are individual memories and in any case, history is always subjective. Some of those I talked too concentrated on the events that they were part of, and they include some of the key moments of the war. Others talked more of their own feelings. Some accounts are dramatic and in some cases, exciting. Others are much quieter, much gentler, but are none the less valid for that, because not infrequently they are about small voyages of self-discovery; of people finding potential in themselves that they did not know they had.

The one theme that emerges, almost throughout, is that people felt that they had gained as much and learnt as much from six years of life in wartime, as they may have lost in other ways. The sense of friendship, the shared endeavour, the bond between people in war, are the qualities mentioned time and again.

Praying to God for strength in adversity, is mentioned relatively rarely. But Christian faith, or at least spiritual beliefs of some kind, may have made a far greater contribution to the sanity and forebearance of those in this book, than I discovered. Perhaps wrongly, the question of God was not one that I touched on, in general.

We are now living in the longest period of peace that this country has ever known. One would prefer to think that peace was productive of the right values and attitudes, that it was a time when some of the ills and injustices of society might be rectified. Sadly, this is not entirely the case. A comment one often hears is "There is so much pressure on people now." These are the pressures of personal ambition, of material competition in a ridiculously fast moving world. Less and less are these considerations tempered by the ideals of service and self sacrifice that were compelled on our parents and grandparents through the experience of war.

On another note, war provided people with an opportunity for adventure, for danger, for taking risks, which is, like it or not, quite often an inherent aspect of the male character. It is to be found in some women too, although the idea of adventure is perhaps more attractive to us than real danger or serious risk as we are programmed more for caring and nurturing than combat and destruction.

It would be both facile and imbecilic to suggest that another war is just what this country needs. We heard enough of that during the Falklands conflict. It hardly needs to be said here, that nuclear weapons have become the dominating influence on our attitude to war .

But history can help to provide us with a perspective on things and can serve to remind us just how great is our fortune to be living in the here and now, whatever the flaws and blots of contemporary life. Something we can do, regardless of our means, our position, our politics, is to remember what superhuman efforts were made, and what a high price was paid to ensure our future.

Compiling this book has been a very humbling experience for me and has made me realise that my life is a very comfortable and rather complacent one. As far as my quest to discover what real survival is about, I found that comradeship, humour, determination, duty, faith, and also, a lack of imagination, can all play their part in keeping people sane under stress. Some of the people I talked to were stretched to the very limit of endurance and are still here today, to tell the tale, forty four years on.

Talking to someone about events that occurred several decades ago, one forgets that this interesting, venerable, grey-haired individual in an armchair, was a young, energetic person in their twenties, on the threshold of life when the war started. It is only when they open their photograph album and you see a young man or woman, looking out at you, that you feel a pang, and you realise just how young they were at the time.

I would like to thank all of those who so kindly gave me their time to share their memories with me. I most sincerely hope that I have managed to do each one of them justice. It is in tribute to them and to all of those who worked , who fought, on sea, on land, or in the air, between 1939 -1945, that I have compiled this book.

Jane Torday

WILLIAM BENSON.

For few, save professional soldiers, can the comradeship of war have been such an extension of the social world in which they lived in peace-time, as it was for the officers and men of the Northumberland Hussars. It seems at times, from William Benson's anecdotal account, as if most of his Northumbrian friends and contemporaries were traversing the rugged terrain of Greece and feeling almost as at home there as they did on the hunting field at home. Here was the old county at war. The Northumberland Hussars, a long established Yeomanry regiment, replicated in its ranks the social structure of rural Northumberland, and approached war with the spirit and elan of a past age, but with the weapons of the mid twentieth century.This combination proved to make not only a gallant but a most efficient and formidable military unit.

This is an account of war experiences at once perceptive, goodhumoured and witty: one doesn't complain of hardships but one does one's bit to be comfortable when the opportunity offers. The Hussars do their duty and do it well (they fought in British campaigns on the Western Front) but such cavaliers aren't inclined to be impressed by a visit from a Cromwellian like General Montgomery; and ironic understatement glosses over the dangers faced.

WILLIAM BENSON.

I joined the Yeomanry very young, in 1924, as a territorial officer. The Northumberland Hussars were just a very good club to belong to.

When the war started I was senior subaltern. On September 3rd 1939, after enrolling the men in Newcastle, I drove to Gosforth Park where we were to be stationed for the first few weeks of the war. I didn't know what to expect, but when I got there, I enquired if there was anywhere that I could get something to eat and I was directed to the Jockey's Room, where I had half a bottle of champagne and an extremely good dinner, all organised by Copper Blackett, who was  Adjutant to the regiment.

We were a cavalry regiment and we went to to Thornton Le Dale in Yorkshire, for our horses. They sent the Cavalry Division to Palestine later, but as were an unbrigaded battalion, we were left behind. We were told that we had three choices; if we chose to be anti-tank gunners, then the regiment would not be split, whereas if we chose one of the other options, we could form two regiments. So we chose to be anti-tank.

Looking back on it, it was absolute madness to think that a cavalry regiment was of any use in modern warfare.The cavalry division of the Hussars in Palestine was eventually converted to tanks.

There was only one cavalry division in the German Army and they were used in Russia, mainly in the forests, where they were probably effective.

We had to ajust to being an anti-tank regiment, but we managed to hold on to some of our, army horses for a time, and we sent them to Mr Young's yard at Melton Mowbray. We kept them until February 1940. They were looked after by soldier grooms and as they were army horses, when we hunted on them, we hunted in uniform. We hunted with the Quorn and the Cottesmore to fill in the time.

It was out hunting that I came as near to death as I ever got in the war. The very first day we went out, it was to a meet with the Cottesmore just south of Melton. We set out and we came to this rather inviting fence. Now I was used to hunting in Northumberland and this part of the world. When I sailed over this jump in Leicestershire, I was not expecting to land in a gigantic ditch on the other side. There was a woman beind me on her horse, and she jumped right over the top of me; her horse's hoof just clipped the top of my hat, knocking it off and narrowly missing my head.. If the hoof had caught my head, I would have been killed. As this woman landed, I heard her say, "By God, I've killed the Bugger!" But she didn't stop.

I held on to my horse and remounted and continued on with the hunt, coming back over the same fence again a few hours later, and picking up my hat as I went past.

I was lucky once or twice during the war. A German tank had a crack at me in North Africa; hit our truck, but managed to miss everyone in it.

There was a particular kind of anti-tank gun that we used in the desert, the portee gun, two pounders and six pounders. The portee was the uncovered chassis of a three ton lorry to which the guns were attached. They were light and manoeuvrable, but offered no protection at all. You couldn't destroy a tank with these guns, but you could inflict damage.

All the original , regular regiments in the Middle East were extremely well trained, and jolly lucky they were, otherwise we would have lost Egypt.

I wasn't in the desert with Monty, but I was with him in Normandy. The only time I ever spoke to him was when he came to inspect us at Chippenham Park near Newmarket. I was in charge, and he said, "Let me see. Who is commanding you?" I told him it was Colonel Mathews. "Why isn't he here then?" he asked. So I said, which was a lie of course, "Oh he's away on leave." Well, the General who commanded the 50th Division overheard this and came rushing back. "Why isn't Colonel Mathews here? I know that he's not on leave."

So being truthful this time , I said "Well, he couldn't be bothered to come. He's fed up with these sort of things." I didn't like to add that he was probably in the bar drinking gin and tonics. There was a grunt and they walked away.

I don't think that Monty was a very pleasant man but there is
no doubt that he sold himself to the troops. He sorted people
out, but how popular he was with his contemporaries, I don't
know.

Wavell, on the other hand, was a very quiet man. My brother
John worked with him. One one occasion they were playing golf
together, and the chap behind them teed off too quickly and
hit Wavell with his golf ball. So my brother John went up to
this man and said, "You've hit the Commander in Chief." This
man got the most frightful wind up. Then Wavell said to my
brother, "You'd no right to  say that'You hit the C.in C.'You
should have said that'You hit my partner.'You've put the man
in the most frightful tizzy."

Early in 1941, we left for Greece and we were there for about
a month until the Germans kicked us out.

When we were in Greece, C Battery, commanded by John Cookson,
was on the Odessa Line, before the Germans invaded. The thing
about John Cookson was, that he didn't give a damn for anybody.
One Sunday afternoon, after lunch, John Cookson was asleep
he'd probably had a  good lunch - when Sir Anthony Eden and
Sir John Dill arrived unexpectedly.  Hughie Northumberland ,
who was also an officer in the Hussars, went in to John Cookson
and said "Wake up John. The Foreign Secretary and the Vice Chief
of Staff would like to see you." Well, John was half asleep
and he didn't see these two figures in the doorway behind John
Cookson, so he said "Oh tell the buggers to go to Hell will
you!"

Later, they all laughed about it and it ended up a good· joke.
John Cookson's father was very similar and there is a story from
the first war that he`had a trooper run up in front of him for
stealing a chicken, when they were serving in France. He said to
the trooper, "This is a very serious offence, stealing food from
our Allies. Anyway, what do you do in civil life?" So the trooper
said, "Please Sir, I'm a draughtsman." To which John Cookson's
father replied, "Well, how would you like it if someone came and
stole your bloody draughts."

Anyway, there was a sequel to this visit from Anthony Eden,
because the Duchess of Northumberland had given him a letter in

England to deliver to her son Hughie. When they all met that Sunday afternoon, Anthony Eden forgot about this letter. A month later, after the Germans had invaded, Anthony Eden remembered the letter and arranged for a special dispatch rider to take it all the way from Athens to C Battery headquarters, about 300 miles .

There was a battle going on at the time, but nonetheless, Hughie Northumberland was found, and this letter finally delivered to him. But when he opened this important communication, it wasn't from his mother at all. It was from the kennel huntsman of the Percy Hounds on a small point concerning the pedigree of a bitch he was intending to breed from!

Greece was my first actual experience of the war. We were detached from the regiment and attached to the Greek Army.We were told to go and hold on to some pass, almost on the Albanian border. Old Dick Rogers was in command and I was second in command, and we had to discuss how to hold on to this pass with the Greek officers. It was all very difficult as they couldn't speak any English and we couldn't speak any Greek. So eventually, over a cup of this very sticky, black, Turkish coffee, we talked French to each other, and I don't know whose French was worse. Anyway, it didn't matter very much as the Greeks hopped off the next day, then the Germans came, and we retired after  that.

On another occasion during the campaign in Greece, we were fighting a rearguard action. We had been badly shot up and had only four Bofars guns for cover, so we had to go very, very, carefully. I saw a cloud of dust and thought that it was probably a German armoured car but when I looked through my field glasses, I saw that it was a Bofars gun. So I went up to it, and who should it be, but Nicholas Straker, who had grown up at Newbrough Lodge just down the road from here. It turned out he had dinner at my home in Newbrough six weeks previously and he was able to give me some news. Nicholas Straker wrote home to his mother that the good thing about all these military retreats was that you bumped into so many people you knew.

That sort of thing , these chance meetings in rather unexpected places, did happen in wartime. These occasions have perhaps stayed more in one's mind than than the battles themselves. I remember in November 1942, my battery was attached to the 12th Lancers who were doing reconnaissance work in armoured cars and were miles ahead of the British army. The 7th armoured division were being relieved by the first armoured division and we were getting a new commanding officer. So when two figures appeared to see me, neither of whom, I knew, I thought that one of them must be our new Brigadier. But his opening remark was , "I had dinner with your sister two months ago; then the other one said, "Yes, we were both there, and so was Adela (who became my wife after the war). This kind of thing happened to everyone, but when you think of the scale of the war it was extraordinary.

After a short period of action in Greece, we had to evacuate. It was the third evacuation of our troops since the start of the war. They had to get 50,000 troops out of Greece. We were supposed to be evacuated to Crete. We set out on one of the boats and this rather nice old boy, Eyton LLoyd, a padre from Alnwick, said that as it was Sunday, he thought it would be rather nice to hold a service to thank God for our deliverance.He had managed to borrow the captain's cabin for the purpose. As we didn't want to upset the old boy, about six of us went: Hughie Northumberland, Dick Taylor, Dick Browne-Swinburne, John Cookson and myself.

We thanked God, and God was jolly kind, because he sent a German aeroplane over and dropped a bomb on us. It missed us, but landed in the water a few yards off the bow of the boat, and knocked a great hole in the side. The captain said, "No Crete, no Crete. We go staight to Alexandria." And that saved us. We never went to Crete but the other half of the regiment who did, were all either killed or captured.

My brother John had a slightly similar experience, a narrow squeak on a boat. He was in the Black Watch and he was wounded on the break out from Tobruk. There wasn't a hospital ship available and they put the wounded on to an ordinary cargo ship from Tobruk to Alexandria, including my brother and another chap called Blair. John was wounded in the leg but the surgeon luckily decided not to put it in a splint. At one point on the journey, when John was down below in the ship, he felt the need to relieve nature and he and this chap Blair both scrambled up on to the deck.

At that very moment, the boat was hit by a torpedo. If my brother and Blair had been down below, they would have been killed. Instead, they were flung into the water and were there for about four hours before being rescued by a British destroyer. My brother is an exceptionally tall man and as the sailors pulled him in from the sea, one said to another, "By, this is a long bugger isn't it!"

He was wounded in November and the following February, when I was in Palestine, I had a letter from my mother ticking me off for not letting her know about my brother - but I had no idea that he'd been wounded.

Having red hair and the skin that goes with it, I got very bad desert sores when I was out in North Africa. I got terribly burnt and the skin went sceptic. They didn't have the medicine to deal with it then. I was in such a mess that they sent me to Jerusalem on leave - not to the flesh pots of Cairo.

Life in Cairo was very agreeable. Philip Pease, who was with us, had a very comfortable flat there where we went to stay.Some people maintained a more comfortable lifestyle in war time than others. It was quite unecessary to make yourself uncomfortable, which some people did.

James, the butler from the Northern Counties Club, came out and started as corporal to one of the squadrons. He eventually became Mess Sergeant to the whole regiment.

Going back to Greece again, I remember that James was with us at Thermopylae, where we were attached to a New Zealand Battalion. On this occasion, the New Zealand commander and myself were sitting in a slit trench, being shelled. James was about a hundred yards away from the action with the mess trucks, and when there was a lull in the shelling, I said to the Commander, "I could do with a whisky." and he said, "I could do with one too."

So I shouted out, "James, bring over a couple of whiskies." James always did things in the correct manner, whether we were engaged in battle or not. He did not have a silver salver to hand, but he bore our whiskies over to us on a tin lid, with due ceremony.

Later, James was badly wounded in Normandy. Eventually, he went back to the Northern Counties Club. He died there of a heart attack, a few years ago, at a Recorders' Club Dinner.

The Noodles, as the Northumberland Hussars are known, were not at Dunkirk, and they did not do Wavell's France , amongst other things. But I think that they saw as much active service as anybody during the war. I should think that the only regiment who saw more, were the 11th Hussars.

Hughie Northumberland was with us when the news came through that his elder brother had keen killed. The Army did try to take care of their dukes, although they were sent into action and that always carried a risk, as can be seen in this case. So when Hughie, as the new duke, got sandfly fever in the desert, he was sent home. They did not want a repetition.

In the second war, the army tried to make sure that brothers from the same family would not be sent into the same field of action, face the same risks. They had made that mistake in the first war, by recruiting people from one area and sending them to the same battlefront. The result was that perhaps every family in the county might lose a son, or all their sons. The reinforcements too, were drawn from the same area. They didn't make that mistake in the second war, but even so, as far as the territorial soldiers were concerned, being very local organisations, they couldn't entirely prevent it.


When the war ended, I was over forty, but I came home before it ended, after three years service abroad, as I was solely responsible for various family businesses at home; a farm, and the Limestone Quarry at Fourstones. My father had died when I was seventeen and then my elder brother who was in the army, had died agerd nineteen, from polio. So I was the only member of the family who could do anything about these concerns.

When I came home from the war, the farm was fine but the lime Quarry business was in the most awful shambles. I had left the foreman in charge and my mother had to sign all the cheques. I ought to have made some other more business like arrangement. Now the whole place is filled up, the quarry and everything.

I travelled home on my own, not with the regiment. I arrived at Carlisle and took the local train to Fourstones. I telephoned my mother from the station and said, "I'm home. Can I have some breakfast?"

I walked up to my farm, and I suppose feeling rather cheerful to be back, I jumped off a wall there and managed to sprain my ankle. I had come safely through several years in action, and this was the first thing that happened when I got home.

The next day, I had to travel to London, and wearing my overseas uniform, I arrived at the station. Two military police spotted me, lame and in my uniform. Luckily, they thought that I had been wounded, so they escorted me to a first class carriage where I was looked after very well.

I didn't marry until after the war. While we were away, in the war, I don't think that we talked about women very much. But there is no doubt about it , that the war broke up an awful lot of marriages. Husbands and wives being parted for three or four years meant that either party might get themselves into trouble. It is human nature. People were young then, and it was along time to be separated. For anyone who had been a POW for four or five years, it must have been even worse. A neighbour of mine here was captured at Dunkirk, and when he came home at the end of the war, he found that his wife had left him. I think that he was probably quite relieved!

After the war, I left the Yeomanry, finishing as a Major. In wartime, the army was enormous, but afterwards, it was much reduced, and if all officers had maintained their station, there would have been far too many of them.If you had been a wartime Colonel of a Battalion, and your job was changed after the war, you automatically went back to being a major. If I had rejoined, I would have returned to being a captain.

Luckily, I don't think that another total war is possible, or if there were a war, it would be total, but it would not be a war of the armed forces, of fighting men.

JOHN BARRETT M.C.

Like William Benson, John Barrett was an officer in the
Northumberland Hussars, or "the Noodles", the nickname the
regiment has come to regard with affection. Like his fellow
officer, John Barrett fought in the ill-fated Greek campaign.
From the Greek mainland to Crete, from frying pan to fire, the
Hussars were directed to go. On Crete, after bitter fighting,
those who had not succeeded in finding ships to evacuate them,
were ordered to surrender. For the regiment, the war had a long
way to run: North Africa, France and on to final victory. For
John Barrett and his fellow captives, fighting ended with one of
its most hard fought episodes and his war, was, thereafter, four
years as a prisoner. His attitude towards both his active
war,(what and who makes a good soldier "once the bullets start to
fly) and his necessarily passive war (does being a prisoner
relieve the pressures of life?) is thoughtful. If P.O.W.s are
sometimes divided into the escapers and self-improvers (see Joe
Kayll's account of his captivity) John Barrett bridged the
divide, doing his tunnelling and preparing for his peacetime
career as well.

JOHN   BARRETT M.C.

I'm not quite sure why I chose to go into the Noodles, but I did.
I was commissioned in 1938. Before the war started, I had also
spent a year at Newcastle University studying mining engineering,
which was my father's profession and also one which I had a
natural inclination for.

When my squadron, B Squadron, was first sent abroad, we ended up
in Egypt. We painted our trucks yellow for camouflage. We adapted
to doing excercises in the desert and always getting sand into
absolutely everything. When you are young, you get used to
anything.

When the Germans threatened to invade Greece in 1941,we painted
our  yellow trucks green to blend with the Greek countryside. We
had Bofars guns in Egypt but then for Greece, we changed over to
anti-tank guns. Three other Noodle squadrons went to Greece
before we got there.

We managed to spend a little time in Athens looking round. I
remember that we all took our evening blues in tin trunks to
Athens, although in the circumstances, it did not seem very
likely that they would be needed.

We were sent up to the North of Greece, where my engagement with
the Germans, the only action I saw on the Greek mainland, was
guarding the Metamorphos Pass. It was the most beautiful
situation, with Mount Olympus just behind it. B Squadron was
given this job while the others who had been there several weeks
before us, retired through the pass.

I can remember Colonel Waller, and I think Billy Benson too,
coming to see me, and where my guns were placed over this 100
yard wide ravine. Having seen where the guns were, Colonel Waller
seemed well satisfied, but as he walked away, he said, "Now John,
it's last man, last round!" Fortunately, that didn't happen.
There were no tanks around, but some armoured infantry carriers
arrived and let fly with some Bren guns. By nightfall, we were
told that we could retire.

Something I did a certain amount of in Greece, was standing in for the dispatch rider,who was suffering from exhaustion.It was pretty tough going bouncing over the rough tracks and roads and not helped by the fact that I was endlessly being dive-bombed,which is what most of my war seemed to be about.

After guarding the Metamorphos Pass, our remaining time in Greece seemed to be mainly one long retreat. Other squadrons fought a few rearguard actions but I was not involved .

When we evacuated from Greece, I was in that part of the regiment that went to Crete. My Battery Commander, Dickie Rogerson, was in command. We landed equipped with Bren guns. I was a lieutenant, aged nineteen, and put in command of B squadron, about 80 or 90 men.

We were given a section of the main road to the Akrotiri Peninsular. When the battle started, we could see very well from this peninsular, because we were looking down and over Maleme Aerodrome, where the parachutists, lots and lots of them, were landing and the troop carrier planes were coming in over the sea. We had a marvellous view. But we did rather wonder what was going to happen to us, because we were just sitting there doing nothing.

Then quite suddenly one morning, just after breakfast, about a dozen German glider planes came swooping down on us and landed all round us. We knew it was going to be difficult. We knew there were more Germans on the way. But it was a bit of excitement.

One of the German gliders landed just beside our farmhouse and one of my section leaders, Wilkinson, had seen it land and wondered what action we should take. So we had a look at it. Now Wilkinson somehow managed to have a grenade on him; where on earth he had got it from I don't know, but this wasn't the time to ask questions.

So I proposed that I should crawl up the wall by the farmhouse, and fling the grenade at the glider, and that my section leader Wilkinson would be covering the glider with a gun and he would shoot the Germans as they ran. That was exactly what happened. The glider was very close to the wall, just a few yards away on the other side, and I was able to throw the grenade so it landed on target.

The glider took light and Wilkinson shot their machine gunner with his Bren gun. The rest of them gave themselves up, including the captain of the whole glider troops, who happened to be among them. So it was quite a fortunate capture. (John Barrett won an MC for this act of daring.)

There were about a dozen men. Armed to the teeth they were, with Tommy guns, spandaus, grenades, all sorts. I immediately armed myself with a tommy gun. We got a machine gun too, which we let off at the rocks over which other gliders approached. It was such fun using German arms and ammunition. You didn't have to be economical in their use - you just let fly.

We had a job to bury any dead Germans as on Crete the terrain is largely solid rock. I was discussing this problem with Laurie Pumphrey, on how we could best dispose of them, when we had one of our frequent visits from a German bomber. It dropped a bomb nearby and blew a great crater in the rocky ground. We looked at each other and said, "There you are." Problem solved.

We sustained our resistance in Crete for twelve days, but after that, the odds were too heavily stacked against us and our retreat accross the island became inevitable. More and more Germans were landing, we had inadequate weapons, no air support and we were up against fifteen thousand well equipped enemy airborne fighters who were well protected by their air forces. We fought rearguard actions to the south of the island, but it was obvious that we were going to be overrun.

We marched for miles over the island. There was almost no food to be had. But our main problem was water. There wasn't any. except what we could get from very dirty wells, and although I did not see much of it, men can behave like animals in those circumstances. An occasional source of water was a broken-down truck, and men drank water from the radiator.

It is funny how it was very often the characters who were the most difficult, or sometimes untrustworthy , or misbehaved, who, once the bullets started to fly, became the most useful. Whereas those who were normally considered to be useful and good did not always prove to be so in those circumstances.

On 27th May, General Freyberg decided that evacuation was inevitable. Morale by that stage was extremely low and we were debilitated and exhausted. The evacuation was extremely tricky and fraught with set backs as all forms of transport were under constant attack. We did not all succeed in getting off Crete and Major Rogerson, and Lieutenants Norton, Milburn, Pumphrey, Arnold and myself were given orders to "make contact with the enemy and to capitualte," together with 212 other ranks.

The officers were flown to Athens and then taken to Salonika, for six weeks. The conditions were appalling there, and the food non-existent. Our huts were full of bed bugs, so we used to sleep outside on the ground, which was far cleaner. We weren't allowed to of course, but it was alright if you kept yourself well down. The troops who guarded us were non-front line, ill disciplined and a fairly bloody lot.

One of the worst experiences of my life was being put into a cattle truck with about twenty or thirty other people and driven by rail for about five days in hot July weather.There was not enough room for us all to lie down at once. There were no sanitary arrangements and we were let out twice a day for five minutes.There were about thirty six of us in the truck and whenever we remained stationary, it was always in the full sun.

That was horrid, and after that I did find it very difficult to feel generous towards the Germans, if they could treat people in that way. But Oh, we survived. It is amazing what human beings can endure. Although I think that when you are young, you can get used to almost anything.

We were taken to Lubeck prison camp. There was nobody there but us, and no food. We spent a year there and that was a very down period, very miserable. There was nothing to eat. There was nothing to do. It was a time of boredom and discomfort. We didn't get any parcels that year. We heard no news. A few letters got through to us but they were always heavily censored, with much crossed out.

Then we were taken to Warburg. Things really started to look up from that point. It seemed unbelievably civilised in comparison to Lubeck. There was food, there were clothes, parcels got through, and things in general were properly organised.

After eating properly for the first time in over a year, I was extremely sick. Once I was able to enjoy my food again, I can remember that one of our favourite things was spam, dipped in sugar and fried.

There were a lot of prisoners who had been taken in France there, including your father, who was responsible for the distribution of news from the camp radio throughout the huts every night.That was the highlight of our day.(Jane Torday's father, Roger Mortimer, was a POW from '40 - '45).

The other information that your father used to pass on to me was the bookmakers prices of the horses in the Classics. We all relied on him to give us the right prices it gave us a bit of fun in a small way. I was much younger than your father, one of the youngest in the camp. We young ones were always known as the 'Nursery'!

Our morale went up by leaps and bounds at Warburg. Life really started looking up. The were books to read. One could send home for books on particular subjects and there was plenty of time in which to study.I was able to restart my study of mining engineering.

I had always had an ambition to train horses for point to points,and I managed to get books on the subject and learn all about it, on paper, while I was in prison. After the war, I achieved that ambition and did train horses quite successfully.

I was pretty keen on escaping too, and I enjoyed all the tasks involved in planning an escape from making maps to digging the tunnels. We worked on a big tunnel at Warburg and we used to deposit the spoil under the coal for the cookhouse. The Germans must have thought their cooks very economical with coal, as the pile never went down. When it got to the point that this had to stop, we filled our pockets with the spoil and dropped it round the camp, scuffing it into the ground as we went.

One less pleasant incident at Warburg was when I was put in handcuffs for a week. This was a form of German retaliation to an incident at Dieppe, where the Canadians had captured some Germans and handcuffed them. Why they should have chosen me for this, I don't know. It didn't actually set us back an awful lot because we got hold of some wire, with which we unlocked the handcuffs, and just had to be sharp on the lookout for approaching Germans and clip them back on again. We all got quite good at devising ways of distracting the German's attention. Douglas Bader who was at that camp, used to do extraordinary things with his legs sometimes; unscrewing them and throwing them about, which used to attract the Germans's attention and rather bewilder them.

When the Germans knew that they were going to lose the war, they started to march us from one camp to another, to get us as far away as possible from the relieving forces. At this point we were at a camp called Eichstatt, and as we were being marched to another camp, some American planes flew over and shot us all up and we had to turn back. Your father was there I know, and some of the friends that he had spent the whole war with were killed in that incident.

It was bound to happen in chaos and tumult of war, that from time to time, you were shot by your own people, by your allies.

Not long after this, we were on church parade one Sunday morning and suddenly we heard a lot of shooting going on and we rushed to our huts, the only cover we had. The next thing was that the Americans arrived, driving their tanks into the camp through the wire - a triumphant gesture. We all cheered like mad.

Once the wire was down, we got out of the camp and got ourselves what we could find.....At that point, we were't responsible, as officers, for other men. So any misbehaviour on our part, couldn't be copied by our troops.

A few days later we were flown home. As we flew over the coastline into England, we looked down and saw an awful lot of bonfires blazing away, and we thought how nice it was that we should be given such a welcome home. When we landed, just North of London. we discovered that in fact it was VE day.

My father met me at Newcastle Station. When I said "Where's Mum?" he said, "She couldn't bear it." It would have been too emotional.

She met me at home at the front door. It was emotional - it was such a great relief to be home again.

As far as being a prisoner of war was concerned, I am quite sure that apart from suffering hunger at some points and indigestion at others, that the experience did me no harm. I am not a particularly nervous person. I didn't suffer from nightmares afterwards. I am not a very imaginative person either, much more of a practical one.

As a prisoner, I had made some very great friends over a period of four years. When any of us meet now, it is usually to remember the amusing times in prison, not the hard ones. But one of them said afterwards, "We had nothing to worry about. No responsibilities. We'll never get another chance to live such a relaxed life."

CAPTAIN A.J.BAKER-CRESSWELL, R.N.,D.S.O.

The outbreak of war was a rather different affair for
professional servicemen than it was for civilians. If few
welcomed war, for they appreciated its horrors too well, it was,
nevertheless, what they had been trained for.
Captain Baker-Cresswell, who had joined the Royal Navy in 1919,
began his war with the quiet confidence of one who knew exactly
what to do. His distinguished war-time career included a part in
the negotiations over the French Fleet at Alexandria, Command of
convoys in the Atlantic, and a top job in Naval Intelligence.
It was during his spell as a convoy commander that his capture of
a U boat, complete with Enigma code machine and secret documents,
played a vital part in the decoding of German Intelligence
systems. This was the war of a professional naval officer, six
years out of forty two years of service.

## CAPTAIN J. BAKER CRESSWELL R.N.

I just missed the first war by a couple of months. I joined the Navy in 1919 as a cadet and when I retired in 1961, I was a Captain.

In the nineteen thirties I was senior navigator on HMS Rodney. I did a naval staff course and an RAF staff course before the war, so by the time war was declared I was fully qualified to do almost anything. The war came at exactly the right time for me. I was ready for anything and I'd handled every type of ship except a submarine.

It was obvious there was going to be a war and in July 1939, I was sent to the Mediterranean as Liason Officer between Admiral Cunningham, the naval C.inC., and General Wavell, C.in C. of the Army there.

One of the curious incidents which comes to my mind from that time, in the earlier part of the war, was how we had to deal with the part of the French fleet in Alexandria after France had collapsed. These French ships were due to return to France, but our great worry was that they would join the Germans, which clearly would have meant trouble for us, and we were determined that they wouldn't.

We had a considerable battle fleet in Alexandria and Admiral Cunningham ordered the fleet to train their guns onto the French ships, and the French were told that if they attempted to move, we would fire on them. In consequence, an impasse was created and I was asked by Admiral Cunningham to sort it out.

I got onto the Ambassador, Sir Miles Lampson (who later became Lord Killearn ) who in turn contacted the French Minister. The French Minister got into a terrible state and claimed that this was not his responsibility, and it shows what a magnificent ambassador Lampson was, that he persuaded the minister, in his beautiful French, to come down to Alexandria. I drove him from Cairo to Alexandria, where he and Admiral Willis boarded a French flagship for discussions. After an hour they emerged to tell us, "It is alright. It is peace.", which meant, in other words, that the French would do what they were told. It was an incident that gave us great cause for anxiety at the time, because there were about twelve battleships in the French fleet and they could have caused considerable trouble.

At the same time, I saw that whatever happened in the Mediterranean, it was a side show. The real business of war was going to happen in the Atlantic. I was determined to get home. I had been on shore in Cairo for nearly a year by then and it was late 1940. I tried to persuade Cunningham to let me go back home but he was not at all keen on changing his staff.

However, when I was least expecting it, Cunningham rang me up and offered me a new job to start in twenty four hours time. It seemed that a convoy had to leave Alexandria the following day and both the Commander and the Captain had fallen sick, and would I like the Job? Of course, I accepted and in some haste, had to pack up my life in Cairo, my flat, my car and so on. The next day I set off , with six ships, for Malta.

Odd though it seems now, it was far safer at that point in the war to take the route round the North of Crete than the way round North Africa, where we would have been under greater threat from enemy aircraft.

My ship was the Brecknockshire. We had quite a number of guns, and it was necessary to see that everything worked properly. First, we had a service on board. Then I said, "God helps those who help themselves. We'll go into Action Stations." But as we were preparing everything, we looked up to see a squadron of Italian airforce coming straight for us. It was very fortunate that we were in a condition of Action Stations, and also that I had had defence practices against torpedo-dropping aircraft in peacetime. I knew exactly what to do.

I had quite a big battleship escort, about half a dozen ships of various sorts, including anti-air craft cruisers . I managed to manoeuvre our little group out of the way of the torpedoes. Although the Italians were dropping on us, and we had our anti aircraft guns, no one hit anyone and we got through the incident without injury on either side.

It was an amazing sight as we sailed into Malta, as practically the whole island seemed to be there to greet us, having brought the convoy safely in. Coming through the Italian torpedo attack was my first taste of action in the war, in November 1940.

We left the Breckonshire at Malta. About a year later she was sunk.

Then there was a rather complicated manoeuvre. On his way from Gibraltar, was Admiral Sommerville with a large convoy of ships. also to relieve Malta. Trouble was expected, and we went out from Malta to meet him. It was the most brilliant Mediterranean blue day and as we were cruising along in these perfect conditions, there appeared over the horizon, the whole Italian Battle Fleet.

I was not part of the action as I was only taking passage, but I witnessed it all from the Battleship Ramilles coming fore and astern of one of our most magnificent ships, the HMS Renown, which was the most beautiful and inspiring sight. This confrontation between ourselves and the Italians was infact the last battle fleet action ever fought. Despite this distinction, I don't think that the story of this sea battle has ever been well publicised.

The outcome of the confrontation was that the Italians finally turned and fled back to Italy. Infact, the Italian ships were very fine and were faster than ours. But as a fleet, we didn't think much of them, although individually, there were some very brave men in the Italian navy. They could have been a very fine fleet indeed if they had been properly handled.

I continued on to Gibraltar in the Ramilles and then came home in the old aircraft carrier Argus.

I was now looking for a new job, and I wanted a job at sea, not in an office. I went to the Admiralty to see what was available, and while I was there, bumped into an old friend, Admiral Sir Percy Noble, who I'd served under before. He had just been appointed Cin C. of the Western Approaches. First I congratulated him. Then I asked if he could give me a job. Within three weeks I was appointed Commander of the Destroyer Escort Group in the Atlantic. I had got exactly what I wanted.

The Destroyer that I was on was the Arrow, and my escort group consisted of about fourteen small ships, from destroyers down to trawlers. There were very few regular naval officers in the crew. They were all reservists.. We didn't use the Arrow for very long because she was a mine sweeper and we didn't need mine-sweepers in the Atlantic. But we did need mine-sweepers in the North Sea. So I swopped her for the Bulldog.

Now the odd thing was, that before the second war, we had never really practiced convoys. We were completely unprepared for the sort of war we had to fight. It seems incredible now, when you consider that the main lesson of the first war was that the Germans very nearly won because of their submarines in the Atlantic. You would have thought that we might have learned our lesson.

So I was in command of the escort group with no real rules to follow. We made our own rules. It was the most marvellous opportunity. I had my own little command, almost entirely separate from other naval activity. My job was to protect the convoys crossing the Atlantic, and we were allowed to go as far West as possible before dispersing convoy.

Unless you have experienced being at sea in winter, in the Atlantic, you have no idea just how bad weather can be. It was terrible. We were threatened with far more danger by the weather than from the enemy, very often . On occasion it was so bad that you had to 'heave to' which in a small ship, means going as slow as you possibly can, down to about six knots or so. You have to steer dead straight into the wind. You see these huge waves rearing up in front of you. and you wonder what on earth is going to happen when you get down on the other side of them.
When it got so bad that you had to heave to, you had to disperse the convoy, which happened very rarely. You had to keep the convoy together as much as you could. I had to disperse convoy twice, and then the main thing was to protect your own ship.

Sometimes on the Bulldog, I would be up on the bridge for forty eight hours at a stretch, just conning the ship and keeping her dead into the wind. Although it was a very frightening experience to be in the midst of such terrible storms, you always felt that you were in control and that you would get through it.

When you had escorted your convoy as far west as possible, it dispersed, and ships went on their way to different ports. Then you would join a convoy coming the other way and escort them back again.

In 1941 ,things were so bad in the Atlantic and our losses so terrible, that if they had continued at that rate, it is doubtful whether we could have stayed in the war. From June of that year, our losses dropped dramatically.A number of things combined to improve our fortunes; we aquired more ships, more aircraft, and started to provide better training.

We established a base in Iceland and I started to go out on missions to meet escort groups which involved travelling as far as thirty degrees West, which was further than anyone had ever been before.

In May of that year, I was due to go out to sea to meet a convoy but I only had a very weak escort group because a number of ships had by now been damaged, sometimes simply by weather .At our Iceland base we had an old P.and O. liner that was quite well armed and functioned as an anti-radar ship. These ships were quite hopeless for this purpose and their crews used to call themselves the Suicide Brigade, which indeed they were.

This particular P.and O. ship at Iceland was commanded by an old friend of mine and I told him that I was going out to sea with a reduced escort. I said "You can either go out alone and go as fast as you can and trust to luck, or come with me more slowly and with the protection of our small escort group." He decided to come with us.

This was on 7th May. I managed to borrow a few additional ships for my group, although I did not think much of the ones that I was provided with. They were nothing like as efficient as my own.

I then had great trouble meeting up with this particular convoy, because for a number of reasons they were hopelessly out on their position.

I was leading the convoy, up in the front. I suddenly started to get this feeling , this instinct, that something wasn't quite right. So I decided to turn round and go back through the convoy to see what was going on.

My instinct had been right. Something was going on. When I was half way through the convoy, the ship right ahead of me blew up. I realised that we were under attack by a U Boat.

If you were attacked, the order was that you had to make an emergency turn of 45 degrees. Within an instant, I was in the middle of an entire convoy of ships turning round me.

Well, we defended ourselves and we managed to extract ourselves from the immediate danger and in due course, our little group of ships continued on their journey. We hadn't sunk that U boat. It was badly damaged but I know that it managed to make its way back to Germany.

As we set off again, I signalled to my friend in the P.and O. ship, "Well what do you think of things now?"
He immediately signalled back "I still think I was right to come with you!"

The very next day, we were all cruising along happily and we had gone almost as far as we could safely go on the oil that we had. It was about noon, and I was making the necessary signals to the other ships when, as I was doing so, two of the ships blew up.

I just couldn't believe that this was happening so far to the west, further west than anyone had been before; we had never been attacked as far out as this.

Well, we had a line of ASDIC ships which proceeded the convoy, and we had two wing columns of ships on either side of the convoy. We had a Corvette in the group , which I positioned in one of the wing columns so that if further attacks took place, he would be in an ideal position to counter attack.

That is exactly what happened. This submarine had somehow managed to get through our ASDIC line and attack the starboard wing column.

I was in the middle of the escort line and I could see exactly where the submarine was . Meanwhile, my little corvette had moved out and commenced attack on the U boat and succeeded in immediately making contact with it. He made a very good attack on the U boat and I moved in to make a second attack on it. Just as I did so, there, right ahead of me, the U boat surfaced. One prayed for that sort of thing to happen. One was then in an ideal position to sink it.

The natural instinct was to ram this U boat, coming in with the very sharp pointed bow that a destroyer has. I was just wondering what speed would be the best to carry out this operation and how to effect the most damage on the U boat and the least on ourselves.

As I gave the order to go in at ten knots, an entirely different thought came into my mind — a sudden recollection of something I was told on my staff training course; this was an account of how, in the first war, the Russians had captured the German cruiser Magdaberg and handed her over, complete, to us. Well, complete meant that she had all her intelligence cyphers intact. These were taken over by the British Naval Director of Intelligence, who didn't tell anyone about them. As a result, he was always considered an absolute wizard at predicting what the Germans were going to do. The fact was that he was decyphering all their secrets. His work was absolutely invaluable.

I remembered this as we prepared to ram the U boat out there in front of us, on the surface of the ocean.

The next thing was that the U boat crew started to pour out of the conning tower, and it looked as though they were going to abandon ship. Then I saw that they were all clustering round the gun and I thought, "My Goodness, they're going to fight it out." So I gave orders to open fire on them.

We started to shell them and they, in turn, started to jump overboard. I stopped the shelling and at this point , gave orders to halt the destroyer 100 yards off from the U boat. I turned to the officer on the watch and said, "By God, we'll do a Magdaberg on this U boat."

I assembled some men with arms and dispatched them in a small boat to the U boat, saying "It doesn't matter what else happens. Get on board the submarine as quick as you can and get down inside and capture the cyphers. That's your job."

By now, the U-boat had been completely abandoned. I told the corvette that had carried out the original attack to go and pick up any survivors. By the time our men had got to the U boat, all surviving germans had been collected and were down below in the corvette.

Our men disembarked from their small craft, and just as they did so, a huge wave came crashing down, smashing the small boat to pieces on the deck of the submarine. But that didn't matter - I had told them that the only important thing was to get the cyphers. There were plenty of other small boats at our disposal.

It was a very anxious time. They spent about four hours on the U boat, going down below and then appearing at the conning tower with armfuls of precious information. Waves kept crashing down over the submarine and it could have been easy to slip and drop the cyphers over the side and they would have lost to the occean.

In the end, they got everything and we picked them up from the U boat. That was the only U boat ever to be captured, rather than sunk, during the Second World War.

The U boat was slightly damaged, but we decided to tow it home. As I watched this narrow submarine being tied to the stern of the Bulldog, I felt that it was a moment when history was being made and that it should be recorded. I had a camera, even though we were forbidden to take photographs. I took a photograph all the same, because I felt "I'm making history now. This is something that has never been done before."

We got about half way back to Iceland with the U boat in tow, when a storm blew up and the submarine was labouring a bit and had started to fill fast with water. The only thing to do was to cut the tow wire and let it go. In a way, this was a lucky thing, because if I had brought her back to Iceland, she would have been seen by all sorts of people there and the Germans would have got to know that their cyphers had been captured. As it was, nothing was known about it until years later. It was one of the best kept secrets of the war.

Only three or four senior people in the entire Navy knew the story. I was sworn to secrecy and so were all my men. The amazing thing was that the number of people involved numbered about one hundred, and not one word of it got out anywhere.

We had succeeded in appropriating the German's Enigma code machine intact, and we had secured all kinds of secret books charts, with the result that from then on, we could decypher their signals straight away. From that point, we started to win the Battle of the Atlantic.

The extraordinary thing was that the Battle of the Atlantic was the most important naval action in the whole war, and yet it was fought by no one more senior than a commander.

I wanted to stay on in the Escort Group, but at the end of that year, I was given a completely different job. I was put to work in Naval Intelligence which was part of the Chief of Staff's organisation, with direct access to Churchill. This was the top of the Intelligence tree, and obviously, terribly interesting work. I did this throughout 1942.

At the end of that time I was told that what I was doing in Intelligence was so important, that on no account was I to be moved. But three weeks later, I was sent for again, and told, "We're losing the war because we're not sinking the U boats. We're getting more ships, more aircraft. Will you undertake the training of all the escort groups in the Atlantic?"

I accepted the job, which meant going back to sea of course, which I always preferred. I was told that I could have anything in the way of equipment and so on, that I wanted.
So I looked around, and as my ship, I chose the Philante, owned by Tom Sopwith, and the most beautiful yacht in the world. I took on the training of the escort groups, and I think that more or less the same training system is still used today.

As our methods improved, we started to sink more U boats. At that stage of the war, the Germans could not cope with losses on such a scale. The result was, that by May 1943, we had won the war in the Atlantic.

Max Houghton was C in C., and I always thought that he ought at least to see what went on at sea. I couldn't understand a C.

in C. who was mainly on shore. I took him out once in the
Philante, on one of our excercises. That was the only time he
ever went to sea. But at the end of it, he asked me if he could
have me as his chief of staff. I didn't like the idea at all. I
did not feel that I was the right kind of person. But he
insisted.

So I started work in Derby House, and after three months I
realised that I had not had a single day off, and that I couldn't
possibly stand this. I asked if I could be relieved from the job.
I said, "There's a lot of war to be fought yet, and I'm blowed if
I'm going to die in Derby House!"

I was relieved of my post . They then put me in command of all
the escort forces in the Indian ocean. I went out there, where
there was a good deal happening with  the Japanese, and I found
chaos. We had to arrange a new system altogether. I managed to
take a few of my pet ships from the Atlantic with me, and we
managed to build up an escort system in the Indian Ocean.

We had one or two spectacular successes and ofcourse, it was so
far from home that they never got publicised. Anyway, this was my
final task in the war until the last episode, which was the
invasion of Malaya.

Dickie Mountbatten was the Supremo in the Far East . He was in
charge of the whole thing and it was not entirely a happy story.
I could tell you some tales about it, but I had better not put
them on the record. I had known Dickie Mountbatten since prep
school and even then, it was obvious that he was a manipulative
character. Of course, he had great charm, but he was a very
ambitious man indeed. I remember an occasion before the war, when
he was Fleet Wireless Officer and just before he left, he staged
a demonstration entitled "How Wireless Works". He put it on in a
huge hall and it was attended by everybody from the Admiralty
downwards.

The   demonstration   was   produced   in   the   most   stylish   and
entertaining manner. What was typical of him, was that he had
stage-managed the event so as to leave a final good impression of
himself before he left that post. That was the sort of man he
was.

The end of the war out there was the most dreadful chaos . This huge Armada had been set in motion. They assembled at Madras. One day out from there, the war came to an end. By this time, this great Armada of ships was in full flow, and nothing could be done to stop something on that scale.

The first place I got to was a small port, where I took the surrender. I had one or two torpedo boats with me which we had used for training, so we sent them in commanded by RNVR Lieutenants, excellent people. There were the Japs, waiting there and delighted to have someone taking charge of things.

Shortly after this fairly tidy surrender, all hell was let loose, because the whole fleet arrived. There was the white ensign flying and at the same time, amphibious tanks and God knows what rolling in. The whole thing was completely out of control.

When everything had calmed down, and been reasonably well sorted out, I asked if I could go home. I travelled back on an American coast guard ship, a nice fat, comfortable ship which did me very well. And that, was the end of the war for me.

MAJOR AND MRS T.H.BAKER-CRESSWELL.


As befits a Royal Marine, Tom Baker Cresswell saw action both at
sea and on land. He served on HMS Effingham during the Norwegian
operations of 1940, was in command of a gun turret on HMS Prince
of Wales in pursuit of the Bismarck, and was with the Royal
Marine Commandos during the bitter fighting of the Battle of
Salerno.

Tom Baker Cresswell's brother, a regular amy officer, was killed
at El Alamein, and his wife's account of her journey home from
South Africa with her children to war-time Northumberland, gives
us a glimpse of the discomforts and dangers of war-time travel,
not only accross the sea but in Britain: air-raids, slow trains,
and rail strikes - strikes continued to take place despite the
war. This story has a happy ending - after the war, Tom
Baker-Cresswell married his brother's widow.

MAJOR and MRS T.H. BAKER - CRESSWELL.

As a young Marine, one of the most enjoyable aspects of preparing
for war was that, before you joined your ship, you did several
months pre-embarkation training. Our training , before going on
the Anson, took about three months and involved about three
hundred men. We all got to know each other, and to know what
direction we wanted to go in - whether it was to play platoons,
or commandos, or whatever.

What was rather impressive was that although some of the men were
married, and in some cases had worries about their wives at home
and that sort of thing, I don't think that we had a single
application for compassionate leave. Nobody wanted to lose their
place in the detachment. They all wanted to go together in their
lot.

I started the war as a subaltern on HMS Effingham. We patrolled
the Greenland straits looking for German merchantmen coming back
to Germany. We were also part of the Atlantic convoys. We might
have forty tankers coming accross which had to be protected, and
as we had no ASDIC ships or detecting submarines at that point,
my job, or cruising station, was to be a lookout on the quarter
deck. I used to lie on my stomach on the deck, using my
binoculars to scan around for any enemy submarine which might be
following us.

Effingham then moved on to Norway, where we had quite a lot of
action as there was plenty of bombing going on. As we had an
Admiral of the Fleet on board, Admiral the Earl of Cork and
Orrery, we flew the flag of the Admiral of the Fleet in
action.This was something that hadn't been done since Trafalgar,
almost. Again, my job, , which was For'ard High Angle Control
Officer, was that of watching through my binoculars for enemy
aircraft approaching the ship. As I turned my binoculars, the
guns followed in the same direction. As time went on, we got
reasonably good at turning planes away. You would see the puffs
of smoke coming from our guns, and then you would see the bombs
dropping. I somehow got into the habit of thinking that they
wouldn't come near me, that they would just come down around us
and splash into the sea. But there were some near misses. A bomb
came down on someone, and it went straight down through his
knees. His only injury was the cut he got on his thumb from the

wings of the bomb.

One of the things we had tried to do several times , was to land soldiers at Bodo, but we kept failing because of German air superiority. On the last occasion that we tried, we were going at a speed of about 28 knots and I spent about thirty six continuous hours up in my shooting box watching. We were defeated this time by damage to the ship. Our bottom scraped a rock and there was no way that we could continue.

British troops withdrew from Norway in May 1940. The next month, after the Fall of France, it was decided to take over the French fleets all over the world. The decision that the French had to take themselves, was whether they wanted to join the Free French or acquiesce to the Germans. Rounding up the French was to take the form of surprise action.

I was based at Plymouth at that time. We were given instructions for the French round up at 2 am one morning. We assembled all the French crews, including a few ladies who had been on the smaller craft, and we put them all together on HMS Raleigh. It turned out that none of them wanted to join the Free French, so the next thing was to get them all back to occupied France.

I was given orders to take them up river to the ship, Tuggery Tort, which would transport them to their big destroyer, Triomphant. So, early one morning, with a string of cutters, full of French sailors, and a picket boat, we set out for the Tuggery Tort.

As we boarded Tuggery Tort, we heard the air raid sirens going. I went up on to the bridge to see the captain and tell him my orders, which were to dispatch the French without delay."Ah Yes," he said, "But the standing order here is , no movement is permitted while an air raid warning is on."

Of course, I was in my fighting orders and I had my revolver at my side. I had all these French sailors to deal with, and quickly. So I said, very firmly, "In the name of the King, up-hook and take us." and that worked. He took the French in groups of forty at a time and, on the journey, they would descend into the bar and some of them got rather the worse for wear on wine and you could hear the Marseillaise being sung....

By 1941, I had joined the Prince of Wales. She was a brand new ship, and it was while I was on her that I was part of one of the most dramatic moments of the war.

I was the officer commanding the Royal Marine detachment of 300 men, including the band. We went from Birkenhead up to Scapa Flow, which was a working up period. We pushed ahead with becoming as efficient as possible, as fast as possible. We even attended wardroom lectures in the evening after supper - the sort of thing that was rather unheard of then. But of course, war creates different conditions.

Then the news got round that the Bismarck was going to get out. Our Captain sought permission for us to join the fleet that would go after her, because he felt that we were now sufficiently advanced in training. Permission was received.

I remember the whole thing very vividly. My action station was officer in the Aftermain Armament Control, so I had direct telephone to the officer in the For'ard Armament control. Our job was to submit visual judgement to our controls on the position of any enemy ship; whether it was going parallel to us, or going away, or coming towards us. We also had radar controlled range finders.

It was quite exciting, because we were with HMS Hood . The Admiral was on Hood, and it was up to him to decide how he was going to fight the action. He told the press men that he had on board the Hood before the action, "I've been in the navy for 50 years. I was at Jutland - and one thing I can tell you, is that ever since then, the Germans have always run away.If .I get the chance I'm going straight in to ram them."

We spotted Bismarck and Prince Eugen at about 30,000 yards . They were quite beautiful ships .As soon as the possibility of action became a certainty, the announcement was broadcast, "Action Stations will be in one hour's time. Hands change into clean under-clothing. Do not forget your anti-flak gear." Another announcement followed forty minutes later: "This is your Captain speaking. We are likely to be engaged in about twenty minutes time. I'll just ask the chaplain to say a few words." And after that, away we went, the Hood and the Prince of Wales after Bismarck and Prince Eugen.

We approached with only for'ard guns bearing, which meant that

Hood had only four sixteen inch guns up the front. The normal thing was to take avoiding action, but the Admiral did not do this.

The thing with naval gunfire is that you watch your splash. That is how you measure your success and if it falls short of the target, you poop it up a bit, until you eventually get that target. In this case, that target was poor old Hood. She was not, after all, an armoured ship. She was a fast battle cruiser. She was the victim of plungeing shells on her fo'c'sle which went down to her for'ard magasine, and she blew up.

Traditionally, we should have shared Hood's fate; but the captain, very sensibly, turned away under smoke.

The Hood had been blown clean in half, and she sank immediately. There were only three survivors out of 1,400. The Prince of Wales suffered several direct hits, but I think we succeeded in knocking out Bismarck's main armament controls. She never fired as well again, after we had made contact. We followed her as far as we could until we started to get low on oil and we had to turn back.

Two other ships, the Norfolk and the Suffolk continued to shadow her. Two days later, the chase hotted up. Prince Eugen was on the way to Brest, but the Bismarck had pressed out into the Atlantic. She was torpedoed and badly damaged by aircraft from Ark Royal, then suffered further attacks from King George V and Rodney. Finally, the Dorsetshire sank her.

When we came into Rosyth from chasing the Bismarck, we were cheered all the way in, which was astonishing really, considering we hadn't won the battle. Of course, we had been damaged; we had shots going through our super- structure and we had about forty dead on board but The Prince of Wales survived that encounter.

The day that Bismarck was finally sunk, the Prince of Wales wardroom bar opened that night and everyone raised their glasses to the Bismarck because she had done so very well. In his account of the sinking of the Bismarck, Ludovic Kennedy, who was watching from a destroyer on the side lines, said that when he realised that this beautiful ship had finally gone, he could hardly bear it.

The Prince of Wales went back up to Scapa Flow for repairs. I left her at this point and went as a reinforcement to the Royal Marine Commandos at Sicily. That meant that I didn't have to go to the Far East and I wasn't sunk in the Prince of Wales.She was destroyed by Japanese Aircraft off the east coast of Malaya.

My wife has always held that I have led a charmed life. This was not the case for my brother, who was killed at the Battle of Alamein. He left a wife and two children. After his death, his wife and I started to correspond very regularly with each other. My brother was a bond between us, even though we had probably only met each other half a dozen times before the war.

I was in on the Battle of Salerno in Sicily, but really as a spectator as I hadn't done any of the battle rehearsals. Salerno was a particularly tough one. There is no doubt that it was thought that the Brits and the Americans would be pushed back into the sea. Nobody had made any plans for that.

We should have been there for 48 hours having held the road to Naples to let things through, but we were there for nineteen days. We landed with twenty six officers and we came out with five. The troops about halved . A large number were killed and many were wounded. I was very lucky, a bullet took a small chip out of my ear, but that was all. But it was a very tough period.

On reflection, I think that it is absolutely magnificent that a book about Salerno has been written by one of the marines in the Commando that I was attached to. This man was a Geordie, a conscript at that time and he had had only eight months training. What he, and all of us, were up against were Panzer divisions that had been all through North Africa – really professional soldiers. There we were, putting eighteen year olds against these experienced professionals, in a Commando with perhaps only three regulars in it. While we were fully stretched, the men from the Panzer Divisions used to leave their defensive positions at night and go off somewhere and whoop it up.

After Salerno, we went back into Sicily. There were a few ups and downs, but there were one or two amusing moments as well. The Command that I was with had aquired two huge containers, of gin. The officers drank most of one of them after the Sicily landings. We still had this other container of gin to drink, so we decided to have a party, inviting every we knew out there, including English nurses who were out there. I had also got to know a Battalion of the Black Watch there, which was commanded by another Northumbrian, Major Conyers Baker- Baker. He and I drank pink gins gallore . News of this somehow got home to my mother!

I was home just after Christmas in 1943, on leave. A little after that I was on the Battleship Anson, which was in the same class as the Prince of Wales.

As the war drew to a close, I spent VE Day in Malta and VJ Day in Sydney.

Then I was the first man into Hong Kong. We knew that there were something like 20,000 Japs on the island, peering from behind shutters and wondering what would happen next. I marched into Hong Kong with Sergeant Major Fitzgerald and 2oo men. We opened the gates, let them all out, and took over.

Several years after the war. my wife met Sergeant Major Fitzgerald and remembering the event, she said, "Aren't you the man who marched into Hong Kong with my husband?"

"March into ? - Gawd, you could 'ave 'eard our knees knocking in Singapore!" he said.

We only landed with 200 men or so, because the Marines do so many vital jobs on ship, that they cannot easily be dispensed with. My detachment were on the Kowloon side. Following good military practice, we decided we'd occupy the station. During the course of our patrols, we came accross Whitfield Barracks,reputedly full` of 20,000 Japs behind the wire.

We saw our internees and POWs released . At a camp on the Kowloon side, one of the British officers had collaborated with the Japs. He was naturally not at all popular with among the other officers of his camp. My job was to arrest him, but by this time, he was physically very debilitated and weak. He had to be more or less lifted into the back of the lorry. He had boxes of papers with him which he hoped, I suppose, would prove his innocence. It was pitiful. I don't think that he ever stood trial. I believe that he lived on. The burden of his own conscience would have been punishment in itself.

It is well known what a dreadful condition most of the Far East POWs were in at the end of the war. A number of them were sent to places like South Africa to recuperate for a while, rather than being sent directly home.

I went home on the Anson, which was due in on 31st July 1946. I invited my sister in law down to meet the ship. That was the beginning of the next chapter for me, because three months later we married each other.

MRS BAKER- CRESSWELL.

The basic instinct when things go wrong is to get home. When the war started , my husband, who was a Sapper, was based at the garrison on Mauritius. We were out there with him. After he was killed at the Battle of Alamein, we were in South Africa. I applied for a passage home for myself and the children three times, and each time we were refused. On the fourth application, we were accepted and I was told that on this boat we would be 99% safe and we couldn't do better in wartime. We had a perfectly horrible voyage. We were in a French battleship that couldn't go faster than six knots and if it tried to, it shook you to pieces. From West Africa, we set out in a convoy of about forty ships, which felt quite safe.

We arrived in Glasgow in the rain, with an air raid warning on, and a rail strike. My children, who had been born and brought up in a hot climate came out into this grey English drizzle,and they loved it. They thought it was absolute heaven.

During the war journeys took a long time; it took two days to get from Kings Cross to Northumberland by train. It was a very slow process with endless delays. You had to spend the night in York on the way.

Then we were back home here, with my parents- in- law. There practically wasn't a war up here. I think that the worst thing about it was that it was all such a slog. You never had enough of anything. You were never quite warm. You never had a hot bath. You never had enough clothes. And one queued - quite often for hours for something one didn't really want in the end. That was really the thing. It was all such a slog.

A friend of ours who had triplets only had enough coke to light her stove twice a week. The rest of the time, she had to cook for her family on three small electric rings, one of which was upstairs.

As a matter of fact, this particular friend had what I am sure must have been one of the strangest war experiences for someone living quietly in the country. Every morning, she put her three triplets out in the garden in their three prams, for a sleep. One particular morning, they all woke up earlier than usual and started to cry. So she thought she might as well bring them in and give them their lunch.

Three minutes after she had carried them in, a German fighter plane came over and machine gunned the row of prams in the garden. The bedding and the prams were full of bullet holes. It was an act of sheer spite.

But talk about a charmed life - or three lives in this case. They only just missed a dreadful fate.

As he said, I've always maintained that my husband has led a charmed life. He came through some of the most dangerous action in the last war, more or less unscathed. I didn't know him well before the war, but I think that all the experiences he had in the war did change him, totally and completely. He started as one person, and finished up as another. I think that the answer is that he grew up.

Once, when we were talking to a friend about our children, he said to us. "You know, I'm really sorry for our kids, because they've never known the experience of war."
What he was talking about was the fact that you are all in it together , it brings certain qualities out in people and creates a terrific bond between them . But of course, I hope that my children and my grand-children will never have that experience.

JACK BRUNTON

Jack Brunton was one of those for whom the war destroyed career
opportunities, taking him away from his night-school studies to
become an architect. Without any ambition for promotion in the
army, the war to him was something to be endured. He adapted
skillfully and with humour, to the hardships of army life and to
its occasional petty injustice˗˙ if the opportunity to 'win' a
bottle of whisky or extra food arose, then he took it. His
account of his service casts an interesting light on relations
between officers and men in the war-time army: they could be
close, especially between an officer and his driver who were
necessarily much in each other's company. There was enormous
respect for the good officer, but if a certain sense of natural
justice was affronted, then the men could surreptitiously exact
revenge. Reluctant soldier as he was, Jack Brunton shares with
so many others the feeling that his war-time experience had many
positive aspects, especially the sense of companionship.

JACK BRUNTON

I had no ambition in the army. I went in as a gunner and came out as a gunner seven years later. I could have had promotions, but I didn't want to be in a position where other people depended on me, because I was a civilian soldier, not a professional one.

There's three types of soldier: there's the regular soldier who's joined up to do the type of work they were meant to do; there's the part-time territorial who played at soldiers at weekends for the fun of it; then there's the civilian soldiers - the militia. In June 1939, we got our call up papers to join the militia. We were twenty years old. We were in work at the time and we didn't want to go, but we were called up.

A lot of us were looking for future careers in whatever we were doing. Quite a few of us had been going to night school, but there was a fall out after the first year. I had been going to Rutherford College to study architecture for three years, and I worked in the building trade during the day and paid for night school out of my wages. I was going to night school to better my education, which was cancelled as of fifty years ago, in June 1939, when I was called up into the militia.

The whole pattern of my life was changed from that moment. Seven years of our youth were taken from us, which I have never recovered from, in the way that it deprived me of my education. By the time the war finished, I was married and had to make a living.

You see, if people would understand that my generation were born just after the first war, and everyone was still recovering from it; then there was the General Strike in the 'twenties, then in the 'thirties, the Depression. Then, before we could get turned around, the second war started.

When we got our call up papers, it was written on the bottom of the sheet, "It would be advisable to bring an overcoat." Where I lived in Byker, nobody had overcoats because they couldn't afford overcoats. So they issued us with overcoats when they gave us our uniform and we had to take what we could get. They'd say, "You're under six foot, there's your coat." and it was practically trailing on the ground. So we had to alter the coat, which was alright as far as I was concerned, because I'd learnt how to do all these things from my father. My mother had died in her forties, when we were very young.

My father was a terrific man who'd fought in the Boer War and in the Great War. My parents had four children before the '14 - '18 war, and then another four after it. My father looked after all of us. He ran the family like a regiment, and we had to do what we were told. But he turned us out nicely, cooked and washed and sewed for us, read us stories. He made a terrific job of it and I reckon he should have been in the New Year's Honours List every year. So at twenty, I could sew and darn as good as a woman. All my life I've been good at make do and mend, at making something out of nothing.

Some of these soldiers in the militia had been mothered, and they used to come and see me to sew on their buttons and darn their socks. They used to like their clothes pressed, so I bought this electric iron for 7/6d and hired it out for 3d a time. I got my money back. Survival tactics, you see, which were necessary when you were being paid 7/- a week, and after various deductions, including 3d a week for haircuts, you were left with around 5/- a week.

To start with, we were stationed at the Cowgate Infant School in Newcastle. Our C.O. was a broad, well built kind of chap. Well, as it happened, the only toilets were little ones for infants, and our C.O. had terrible trouble with them. We used to look for things like that - they kept us going. Whereas the professional soldier at night would sit and polish his boots, it was so hard for us, and we'd look for these little tit-bits, so we·could smile.

Just after I joined, I had the job of waking this duty officer with a cup of tea at 6 a.m. every morning. Well, one morning I overslept till 6.45. I wasn't that bothered, but as I was going through the wash-house, this Sergeant Major Thompson says, "You were looking after Captain Baker, Where is he this morning? He wasn't on duty." So I says, "He must have slept in.."

I knew I was going to be in trouble because this Thompson had seen us, so I got a cup of tea, drank half of it myself, then

filled it up with cold water. I crept in and put it beside
Captain Baker's bed. Then I said quite loudly, "Oh, you must have
slept in." He was up immediately. "I never sleep in." he says.

"Well, I brought you a cup of tea at six." I said. "There it is."
So he picked it up and ofcourse, it was cold. "I'm so sorry." he
said. And that was that. Well, you've got to do these things.

Out of my seven years in the army, about six and a half were
spent abroad. I was still in England, just after the Fall of
France, based in Bournemouth, on coastal defence. Well, it was a
Dad's Army - completely. I did a guard's duty at a position
guarding one of the main arteries into the middle of Bournemouth,
with a 303 rifle and five rounds of ammunition. Now was I going
to stop the German Army? What could I do, the lowest of the low,
a civilian soldier who was only there until I could get out
again?

We were billeted in this big house on the seafront - beautiful.
The officers were there enjoying the garden, and we could go down
to the beach and sunbathe: twenty mile away accross the channel,
there were eight million Germans.

We had no idea what was going to happen because no one ever told
you anything. We used to get up in the morning and the Commandant
would say, "Right. There's a twenty mile run this morning." And
you just ran into Bournemouth, and the route they had chosen for
you was a bus route, so you'd jump on the bus, get off and read
the morning paper until you thought time was up, jump back on the
bus, then just run the last lap home. And people thought we were
fit, but we'd never done anything. The only time we ran was when
the Germans were after us.

We sailed from Greenock early in 1941. We had cruisers,
destroyers, aircraft càrriers with us - terrific. But the next
morning, we woke up out on the Atlantic and there was not a
cruiser, not a destroyer, nothing in sight. Then we got to know
that the Bismarck was loose. Well, down in the hold, it was all
panics. That night, everyone was up on deck, no one would go
downstairs. We were all too frightened, knowing the Bismarck was
loose. And I should say that it was the first time that ninety
nine per cent of soldiers on that ship had been to sea. They had
never been abroad - nothing. Their life had been spent down the

pits, on building sites. Twenty year old and never been out of their front street practically.

I was lucky. I wasn't sea sick but some lads were terribly ill, they were out on the deck practically praying for a submarine to come and torpedo us and put them out of their misery. Some were literally crying.

Once I was overseas, I started to work as a driver for this officer, Major Baker. I had this lovely Humber Snipe to drive. In Cyprus, after Crete had fallen, we had to drive all over the island and chart every road and by road, as they were going to make it a fortress. I did a lot of hole digging too. By the end of the war, I had dug holes all over the world.

I caught malaria in Cyprus and went to hospital. Then the news came that we were on the move again. I still wasn't too well, but I didn't want to be left behind. I was a young lad, still green, and you cling on to what you know. So I went with them to Palestine, and then a few weeks in Syria, which was interesting.

Just as we were enjoying ourselves after all our hard work in Cyprus, we were told that the Germans were coming round the Caucasus, so we're sent there. Whose brainy idea that was, I don't know, to send us straight from a warm climate into the frozen Caucasus. There was more digging of holes, but we coudln't get into the ground properly, it was that frosted in the middle of winter. We couldn't even get the tent pegs in; we had to hold them down with boulders.

We got drink rations every week; one can of beer for us, and spirit rations for the officers. While we were in the Caucasus, me and this lad were on guard outside the officers mess tent one night. In that tent, they had this bamboo table where they kept the drinks. This night, a strong wind got up and blew the Mess Tent down, knocked over the table with all the drinks, but not one bottle was broken. So I says to this lad, "Terrible that. But I'll tell you what we'll do." So I emptied my water bottle on the ground and filled it up from a whisky bottle. I clipped the whisky bottle to give it the look of a bit of damage. Then this lad and I drank the contents of my water bottle.

The next morning, we were still a bit squiffy and this Lieutenant appeared and said, "It's been that cold, we're going to have a rum ration." He poured mine out and I was feeling that squiffy, I could hardly hold it. "What's the matter?" he says. "I've been on guard and I'm cold." I told him.

After the Russians had curbed the Germans in the Caucasus, we were brought into Iraq for three months - straight from the cold into the heat this time.

Then they sent us into the desert, and I was two years there. First, we were stationed at Gazala, at Divisional H.Q.

It was very, very boring in the desert for a lot of the time; there was nothing to do. But I think that all wars should be fought in the desert, because there's no civilians, no children, no old historic buildings, nothing to be destroyed.

War is terrible, and there's nobody knows what war is unless they've seen it. In the desert, you're sitting with a lad one night and you're sharing a tin of bully beef and as you are eating it, he's whopping the flies off you, and then it's his turn to eat, and you're whopping the flies off him. And the next day, he's dead. And you just put him in a hole and turn him on his side and shovel sand on top of him. Death is sudden and it's definite. There's no time to turn around and say, "How are you keeping?" There were so many that didn't come back.

After fifty years, things dim you know. But you've got time to look back on things. Sometimes you feel this fear that you came back and so many others didn't. Ten thousand of us went out in the 50 Division and about one thousand came back. We lost a whole brigade at the Gazala retreat, three thousand men. Ofcourse, some men were wounded, some transferred and some were taken prisoner, but there's a lot of difference between ten thousand and one one thousand men.

By the time that we were in the desert, this Major Baker had transferred to the Royal Army Service Corps and he was chief Ammunitions Officer for the 50th Northumberland Division and I transferred with him. It was our job to get the ammuntion round the back of the enemy lines - we used to take fifty or sixty wagons of ammunition at a time bend the German and Italian lines and dump them under camouflage.

Now when Montgomery took over, everybody had to have two jobs - a gunner had to know how to drive, and a driver had to know how to cook and so on, then one could take the place of the other if necessary. We got to know a lot more when Montgomery took over, and Horrocks. The rank and file became far better informed than they had been under Ramsden, Kirkup and Graham.

The younger officers seemed a lot easier to get on with. As the war had gone on, other officers had come up from the ranks, rough, tough, and you knew where you were with them. You've only got to think of General Slim. He'd only been a foot soldier in the First War, yet he ended up a Field Marshall in the second one. The men would follow him anywhwere. We had one like that in the desert, Connor, and we would have followed him anywhere. But Auchinleck, Wavell, nobody knew them, nobody had seen them - they might as well have been ghosts.

If you took prisoners in the desert, you could take one on Tuesday and he'd be free on Wednesday, it was that open, very easy to escape. The only way to keep hold of your prisoners was to take their water bottles from them and keep the water tanker moving just in front of the column of prisoners. That way, you could hang on to any number of prisoners, thousands even, with only a few dispatch riders going up and down to guard them. They wouldn't leave the water tanker.

On top of our rations, we used to buy baps and sandwiches from a chap who came round selling them - and they could have been full of anything. But two of us ran short of money for these baps. There was a Major Foster who had four ducks which he was fattening up for Christmas, so we said to the bap-seller, "Would you like to buy some ducks?" Yes, he would. So we we traded them in with him and had free baps for the rest of the time that we were there. And the Major was stomping around looking for his ducks. But you have to do little things like that.

We all had to take turns with the cooking and once when I was on, I put my hand in the tea sack for a handful of tea, and came out with a black scorpion. It bit me on the hand and Major Baker put a tourniquet round my arm, cut a slit in my hand and bled us so the poison would come out. I was under sedation for a few days after that.

Major Baker and I knew each other that well by this time, and I could say anything to him. There was, well, no class distinction between us. When we were in Sicily, we had a bad experience when we found ourselves being stukka dive-bombed, and there's no answer to that. The noise of them coming down is terrifying; we were in a slit trench and Major Baker started to panic, shouting and swearing. I knew him so well, that my answer to this was to quote Rudyard Kipling to him. You know the poem "If you can keep your head when all around are losing theirs and blaming it on you."

I quoted this poem to him, because it's the only poem that dwells in my mind,even though I've read a lot of poetry. There's something about Kipling that gets inside your skin.

And then Major Baker says, "If we get out of this alive, write that down for me."

After the war, the first time we went down to see Major Baker in Cornwall, I bought him a copy of "If", and from then on he kept it hanging over his bed.

I was part of the D Day operations. We landed very late on in the day, by which time it was quiet. It felt a bit like Druridge Bay, sand dunes and grass.We were near that tall,narrow house you always see in the films about D Day.You were supposed to be off your landing craft in three minutes, but there was nothing going on and I had this five hundred weight truck and I had to check something, so I put the bonnet up to have a look. When along comes this little red-faced beach master; his hands were going like windmills and his face was redder than beetroot. He wasn't the size of two pennyworth of copper and he was as round as he was tall. To finish it`off, he had a tin hat on that didn't fit him. And he was in the most terrible temper. Well, he'd likely been there since early morning, but I looked at him and thought, "If you're the beach master - God - how are we going to win this war?"

About four days after the D Day landings, we arrived at this lovely little village - imagine it - called Jerusalem, in the middle of Normandy. It was full of apple orchards, and when they started shelling over us, the vibration from the shells brought the ripe apples showering down from the trees, and I could just put my hand out and catch them, and eat them. That was such a strange thing in the middle of it all - these beautiful apples being showered down on us as a result of the bombing.

Later, we went through the Falaise Gap, which was dreadful. The smell was so bad, you could taste it. There were mounds of dead, rotting farm animals. In France, the walls of the cow byres were made from straw bales, and the cows were tied up. So if a byre was hit and burnt down, the cows were burnt with the byre, and all that was left were their hooves. And as we went through the Falaise Gap, the banks were littered with dead Germans, and by God, they seemed to look huge some of them or perhaps it was because some of them had their great coats on.

Last of all, I was in the Ardennes. By then, we knew the war was going to end. Although I'd been courting since 1939, I always said that I would never get married until the war was finished. Being in the building trade, if I'd had a hand cut off or anything, I wouldn't have been able to make my living. So Major Baker was going to London for four days and he asked me if I'd like to go too.

So I sent a telegram to Margaret, and asked her to take out a special licence. I got up to Newcastle, and wearing my battledress, we were married that Saturday. We took a trip out to a village in Cumbria and on the way, we travelled through a quiet, little village in the Allen Valley which I had never heard of then, but we have lived here for the past thirty two years now.

In wartime, we'd lived more or less in the conditions of a tramp for all those years. I didn't like all the travelling that was forced upon me by the war, but at the same time, I wouldn't have missed it. The terrific thing that you did get out of the war was the companionship. Everyone was in the same boat, and everyone helped each other.

ROBERT FIFE.

One of five brothers, all territorials in the Northumberland
Fusiliers, Bob Fife's account of his war draws our attention to
two aspects of soldiering: the delight many soldiers took in
outwitting the system - "crafty lads" managing to skive and make
themselves comfortable - and how the very same men would often be
the best of soldiers, brave and selfless, when it came to battle.
What also stands out from this gripping account of the Fusiliers
fighting their way into Germany, is Squadron Sergeant Major
Fife's sensible and humane attitude to the German enemy, and
his contempt for the corporal who needlessly humiliates a German
sergeant major who is taken prisoner. He witnessed the surrender
of German troops in the North West (they had agreed to surrender
once the British had advanced to the Baltic and then sealed off
Schleswig - Holstein and the Danish Peninsular from Soviet
penetration), three days before the final, general surrender on
Luneberg Heath.

ROBERT FIFE.


I was one of five brothers and we'd all been territorials in the
Northumberland Fusiliers. It was a record, to have five brothers
in the same regiment.

My brothers and sisters and I grew up in Newcastle. We lived, the
whole family, in two rented rooms. My father had been crippled in
the First War, for which the government gave him four shillings a
week, which they reduced to two shillings, when as a lad, I added
to the family income by bringing in four shilling a week from a
paper round. From that moment, I have always been a very strong
anti-Tory man. Because I will say this, my family were all
workers and my father did the best he could, taking in odd bits
of work, shoe mending and that sort of thing.

My mother was just a little woman, but you know, she was bigger
than anyone in the family. How she worked - cooking and washing
and sewing and cleaning for us all. She kept our uniforms
perfect and we reckoned she could put on puttees better than any
soldier. We were a family and we were one for all and all for
one. We're the same now, in my own family. Everything is to be
shared.

In those days the Territorial Army was run by local businessmen -
the Colonel was from Newcastle Breweries and the Major was from
Andrew's Liver Salts. At that time you couldn't get a job, in
Newcastle Breweries unless you were in the forces. It was run in
that spirit and it worked.

In 1939 I was working for a transport company in the Team Valley,
earning fourpence halfpenny an hour, working forty five hours a
week.

Then I got my call-up papers. At the start of the war, we were
all as excited as could be. We went down to the old Medical
College in Newcastle for our medicals and the whole place stank
of formaldehyde and was full of jars of preserved fingers and
other parts of the body: a great start to our military careers.
The medical was a scream - we all lined up in a row and were
asked to give a small cough and that was it, "Right, you're in."
And there were all sorts, flat feet, colour-blind, short sighted,

deaf — but they were in.

For officers, there was Major Peter Bell, a right horsey man; Colonel Carrick, Major Gardner, Major Criddle, Hey diddle diddle. Then there was Peter Angus, a stunning bloke, real good looking and a real gentleman to boot. You knew those officers who were gentlemen, who knew when to say, when not to say, and all that. Then there was Rex Potter and others; we were all one great big happy family.

It was hilarious at the start because they fed us at a high class restaurant, Lockfarb's at the monument. Well, we'd never seen anything like it in our lives: the linen tablecloths, the cutlery laid out, the best of food, waitress service. After three days, they decided it was too good for us and we landed up at a Salvation Army Hostel after that.

We were stationed in Newcastle for quite a while, guarding things, including all the bridges — but no one knew what they were doing. You didn't know what to guard, but you had to guard it. One man was on guard at the Swing Bridge and I had to go down there: no sign of him, but his gun was propped up against the parapet. I knew where to find him — across the road in the pub. "No one will bother," he says.

But we got organised. Near to the beginning of the war, we were stationed beside the submarine base at Blyth. It was quite an active base. When one of the subs sank a cruiser off the coast of Norway — Well — talk about jungle telegraph — we knew in Blyth about our sub sinking this ship, long before the Admiralty knew about it. How the devil. When the sub came home, we had to provide a guard of honour because the crew was decorated for their exploits.

It was at Blyth that we experienced our first little bit of action, when a bomber came over and started to machine gun the coal boats on the river. It was quite laughable — we were in the drill hall, and we couldn't get under the beds fast enough, hearing this gunfire. But outside, there's this skipper out on the deck of his boat in his pyjamas, shouting and swearing at this bomber and blazing away with his ship's gun at it, for all he was worth. We were supposed to be the brave ones, cowering away under our beds in the drill hall, and here's this skipper taking on this bomber in his pyjamas. Great!

The coal boats from Norway and Denmark used to come into Blyth and we were sent onto the staiths on the north side of the river to guard them, because their soldiers weren't allowed off. But soldiers being soldiers, we got talking, and then they'd say - "Get us a bottle of whisky." and they'd give us a few coppers to go down the town and get the whisky.

Well, we used one of the trimmer's cabins on the staiths as a guardroom. It was lovely and warm, a massive great fire and lots of coal. Well, last thing at night when the last passenger ferry had gone home, you knew that there would be no one accross till morning. Then the cry went up - "Right on Lads. In! Never mind the guards. Shut the gate. All in the cabin with your heads down." And there we all were. Nobody worried about the guards. Everybody was spark out. We had a high old time.

The orderly officer used to come over on the passenger ferry sometimes and try to catch us off our guard, but we got fixed up with the skipper of the ferry. Whenever he crossed the river, he used to blow the horn three times. When he had the orderly officer on board, he used to blow four times. And this orderly officer could never work out why he couldn't catch us. That was how we controlled the wharf.

You see, that was how the mind was working, even then. The crafty lads were getting that crafty - They weren't saying, "I can't do this and I can't do that." They were getting organised, they were wide. Some of the things they got up to, you wouldn't believe it. The escapades. But that is how survivors are made. I mean, some of the stories you had to listen to, you'd say "Never in the world." but it was their story, and you couldn't dispute it. But we are survivors. Nothing will get us down come Hell or high water. And there was plenty of that to come.

In 1940 we went away to train on tanks, to learn to be good tank men. So we trained and we trained, and just as we were starting to feel like battle-hardened veterans, Lo and behold, the army decides that they're going to convert us to a secret weapon. Great. So off we go to Lowther Castle for special training on the C.D.L. tanks invented by a Professor Mitzakis. These tanks would have had a devastating effect in night battles, as they were equipped with very intense flickering light beams, making it impossible for any machine gun to penetrate the source of this blazing light. We were out on the Penrith moors throughout the winter, at night time. It never seemed to stop raining. There was practice and more practice until we were organised with this secret weapon.

I was in the 49th Battalion of the Royal Tank Regiment, but while we were working with the secret weapon, I was in the 79th Armoured Division, known as "The Funnies" because of the unknown weapons we were working with.

Eventually, we were sent to France in 1944, after D Day, with our secret weapon, the C.D.L. tanks. We thought that this was our Great Day at last. But we sat doing nothing for a month; we were right beside the Battle of Caen, and we couldn't do a thing. It was at that late stage that it was decided that those tanks could not be used after all. Our very last chance to use them was the Battle of Falaise, but we weren't used. And as it happened, they didn't manage to close the Falaise Gap and the Germans got away.

Never mind. The next thing we were put onto were Sherman tanks with no turret on called Kangaroos. The idea was that you could fit a whole lot of infantry into a Kangaroo, and a whole troop of Kangaroo tanks could carry a whole company of infantry. You just went Whoosh along the road straight to where the Jerrys were; breaks on, then "Right on Lads – out you get." Then back you go to get another lot.

We took the Kangaroos into Holland and staged an attack that was the first attack of its kind ever carried out by the British Army. That is, that none of the infantry walked into battle. We took them up to the line in our tanks. The fields had been mined, but the tanks got through them, into the town of Venlo. Our casualties were very, very light. Those tanks were the forerunners of the armoured personel carriers.

In late 1944 we went into the Ardennes. It was hilly countryside, covered in snow and ice. The tanks took off like sledges – you had no control, you couldn't stop. You crashed into anything that was in your way.

On Christmas Eve 1940, we arrived at a village in the Ardennes called Flavion. As we went in, the Americans were coming out, couldn't get away fast enough, flinging mines all over the road. Panic!

We went into the village and these RAF lads were there, a Radio Direction Finding Unit . They had decided to sit tight and stay there. They offered to fix us up - all twenty five of us. It was a real welcome. First they gave us a big dixie of tea and slabs of fruit cake. Then they took us down to their depot, gave us some petrol. "You can have a Bomber as well if you like." they said. The plane was just standing there, nobody bothered about it. Back in the village, they had laid out this terrific spread. "Where do you get all this from?" we said. "Oh, the Americans. They just don't know what to do with it. We can draw what we like from them."

Then, although it was sleep we really wanted, there was a dance that Christmas Eve. It seemed crazy, a dance in the Ardennes at that stage of the war. But we joined in, and I met this American and we got talking. I asked him, "Do you know the difference between a British and American tank?" He said to me, "If we see tanks, we bomb them. We carry five hundred pound bombs. Tanks are all the same to us." "Well," I said, "Keep away from me!" Then I said to him, "Anyway, why don't you get yourself a real aeroplane like a Mosquito?" and his exact reply was - "Ahhh - I'd give my left arm for one of them damn Mossis - they fly alongside us then cock a snoop and leave us." What a laugh that American was.

The next thing after that was King Leopold's Palace: the Chateau d'Ardennes, with massive black and gold bathrooms for every bedroom, and in every bedroom, massive beds about ten foot wide. The Germans had just moved out and they hadn't destroyed it in any way. What a marvelous place. We stayed there until the big push, when we headed for the Siegfried Line.

That was when the rough times really started, before we got into Germany proper. We saw action at Eindhoven, Goch and Cleve. We were alright because we were just dropping the infantry off; they were doing all the dirty work. But at Eindhoven, we got caught with our pants down good and proper. Everyone had said that Jerry was beat. He wasn't. He gave us a terrible time there, bombing left, right and centre. That is when we started to lose men and A and F Squadron lost them in every direction.

It is a frightening experience when you hear gun fire and you know a shell is coming your way. You drop down on the floor and try to get as far into the ground as you can. It's laughable really, because you're worming yourself into the ground, and your behind is stuck right up in the air.

Then we went into the Reichswald and that was one of the most nerve-wracking experiences you can get. You go into the forest and they're machine gunning away like mad, and it's in the dark, and the noise is dreadful. And you do get lads screaming for their mothers. But you got through that day and you were on with it the next day again. Some of the lads were on with it that much, they got what you called "bomb happy", which meant that they'd just walk about if they were under fire; they had lost any sense of caution; they just couldn't have cared less any longer. They were walking about with these moaning minnie bombs raining down.

There were other lads who were genuinely frightened to go out, and you couldn't blame them; they'd been through so much. But they were classed as cowards, and to call them cowards was wrong. There were lads in the tank who wouldn't get out - the officer was supposed to draw a revolver on them, but you couldn't do that, you didn't know what they had been through.

The only instance I knew of a lad losing his head, was when a mortar bomb dropped on the tank he was driving and blew the troop sergeant to pieces. The driver wasn't scratched. When he'd taken in what had happened, he jumped out of the tank and ran away as fast as he could down the road. He more or less recovered, but he was very dodgey after that. You couldn't rely on him. We what you call "carried" him after that. We took him around in the tank, and he was happy with that.

When we pushed through the Siegfried Line into Germany early one morning we caught our first Germans shaving, washing, preparing for the day. So it was "In there and get them all. Hands up against the wall." Whilst we're getting this organised, along comes this smartly dressed chap down the road, taking his dog for a walk. So we said, "Right. Come on. In you come. It's a German Surrender here." But No. Could he take his dog back home and join in the surrender later? Dear Me. And there's a roar

-"Come and join the queue!"

Some of the prisoners were just young lads. Well, this corporal
with a red cap walks along this row of young German lads and he's
pacing up and down and shouting at them. He comes to this German
Sergeant Major and he's shouting at him, swearing at him,
"Hitler's a so and so." The German never said nothing. "Where's
your pass?" shouts the Corporal. So the German hands him this
folder with his papers, including photographs of his family, which
the corporal promptly takes out and throws away. Then he hands
the pass back. The German looks straight ahead. And I thought,
"What a fool that corporal has made of himself."

The day after we took those prisoners, there was trouble. I was
messing about with my tank when there was this God Almighty
crash; a shell came and landed, and there lying, was my mate. He
had shrapnel under his heart; I took his beret off and his head
was a mass of blood. So Hell's Flames, how to get him to hospital
as quick as we can - but we get him there and his chances are
fifty/fifty.

We get back, and there's another crash. This time, there's Peter
Angus who was such a good-looking bloke, dead. The shrapnel had
got him. The officer with him had his leg blown off, and I had to
get him sorted out, put a tourniquet on as best I could. Then
Lord Almighty, there's another crash, and one of the sergeants
who was out in the field has been hit. The wound was that big
that I had to shove a whole roll of my first aid dressing into
it.

Now there's me, only twenty three years of age, and I had all
that to put up with. But it didn't stop there. You had to carry
on. And here's something I ponder about when I read the papers
now about all this stress business. A policeman goes to one of
these sieges and the next day, he's suffering from stress: one
instance of stress - but these lads in the war, it was day in,
day out. Nobody bothered about stress then. We were young lads
then, not old men. And we had to put up with it, seeing our mates
blown to bits.

And there's the other point - Bravery. When the shells came over
and one of the lads was hurt, no one wondered about another shell
coming over. All they thought about was helping their mates who

were wounded or whatever, to get out. You were out and doing what you could. That is the type of bravery which isn't recognised at all. I mean, today, a policeman goes up a bridge and talks a man down from the bridge and he gets a citation and a medal. I've often thought how those lads had been as good as anything, yet very few of them got recognised. There were colonels who automatically got the DSO; there was one at Catterick Camp who'd never seen action. It was wrong. You've got to be in action to know what it's like, to understand what it's like to be frightened.

One time on the advance into Germany, there was a unit in the Essex Regiment who had been pinned down in the woods, in the rain, and their rations were down to nothing. We were asked if we could get some food through to them in the tank. So we got trays of sausages and bacon, and some tea, and two of us went in the tank and found them in slit trenches, half full of water, soaking. So I said "Right. Get your trousers off." and I started the tank engines up while they stood there in their shorts. I hung their trousers on the back of the tank and the engines were that powerful, they were dry in ten minutes.

The lads were ever so grateful and we gave them half a gallon of rum to keep them going. Now these lads had all this to cope with, then people who don't know turn round and call some of them cowards. How much has a man got to put up with?

One of the worst patches was round Bremen. We were waiting outside Bremen to go in and sort things out. It was a lovely sunny day and we were lying around in the sun, just waiting for the right moment to go in, when they decided to send a thousand bombers over the town. We were sunbathing and at the same time, watching these bombers drop ten ton bombs. You could see them as clear as could be.

We went past Bremen, towards Cuxhaven, and that's when it really hotted up for us. We didn't know at the time, but Himmler was in Cuxhaven. Naturally, he had his best SS people with him. We started to come under really heavy shelling and things did get really tough. We were on the attack, going forward, looking for trouble. We would be two or three days on the go like this — then there would be a lull — then it would start all over again. As we were the tanks transporting the infantry, we were up at the front line most of the time.

Between November 1944 and the end of the war, we went into action thirty six times, inside of six months. It is an awful lot. We worked out our chances of not being killed and they were four to one. If you go into action thirty six times at four to one, the odds are against you all the time.

We were at Reisenbech when the war ended. For our billet, we took over this lovely little inn, great for the Sergeant's Mess. We sent the German family who owned it accross the road to put up in their barn.

But it was bitterly cold, so I say to the officer in charge, "It's not right. There's plenty of room here for all of us." So he says, "I want to know nothing about it. There's a non-fraternisation ban on. Be it on your head if something goes wrong."

Do you know, it is the best thing we could have done. We would get back to the inn at dinner time and instead of finding a tip, we'd find the beds made, clothes washed and ironed and mended, everything in order.

One day, I went into the cookhouse where one of our lads was preparing the food, and the old Frau was standing there, pointing at him, saying "Keine gut Koch. Keine gut." (Not a good cook. No good.) So I say, "Du kuchst besser?" (You cook better?) And the next thing was, she took over. I've never known anything like the life after that. We had eggs, butter, cheese, pork, venison, german sausage, cakes. If anyone had seen the way that we lived, there would have been murder on.

To be honest, I've always liked the Germans. I didn't feel any animosity towards them. When you got talking you discovered why they had supported Hitler. He'd given them hope and opportunity and a far better standard of living than they had had before. Of course, we didn't know yet about the real evil of Hitler at that time - the concentration camps.

Germans are very clean, orderly people and I find them easy to get on with. I have been back to Reisenbech since the war.

Finally, there's a little bit of history we've never been credited with. At the beginning of May, when we were in the Cuxhaven area, I was stationary in my tank, on the road. I saw some figures walking up the road in our direction. As they came closer, I could see it was a party of German generals and one German naval officer, Admiral von Freideberg in a black coat. I recognised him from photographs in the paper. Some of our officers went up to meet them. The German officers carried a white flag. They stood discussing things together, near my tank. How I wished I had had a camera at that moment.

The surrender was signed three days later, but it had all taken place already outside my tank at Cuxhaven. I have never seen anything about it in any recorded history, and I read a lot. But I wrote it up in my diary in 1945, when it happened.

JOE KAYLL.

Joe Kayll's war came in two sharply and suddenly divided parts.
Only for an airman could the war bring breakfast in Britain,
and supper as a Prisoner of War. Flight Lieutenant in the
Auxiliary Airforce at the beginning of the war, Joe Kayll had
seen service in France, had flown throughout the Battle of
Britain, graduated from bi-planes to Hurricanes and been promoted
to Wing Commander, when he was shot down during a daylight raid
over France. No greater contrast can exist than between the life
of action, excitement and danger that was the lot of the fighter
pilot, and the sedentary and confined existence of a P.O.W. This
perhaps explains, along with the fact that airmen tended on
average to be young and for the most part, unmarried, why so many
in the R.A.F. camps attempted to escape. Joe Kayll was head of
the escape committee in his camp and involved in one of the most
famous escapes of World War 11.

JOE KAYLL.


I had always been fascinated by aeroplanes. As a boy I used to get hold of all the aircraft catalogues and that sort of thing. Flying appealed to me far more than joining the Territorials. I first applied to join the Auxiliary Airforce when I was nineteen, but was told that I was too young and to come back a year later.

It was a new squadron and I was the third young man to join. Dudley Craig and John Sample were also in it. We had a first class training and there was tremendous keeness. I don't think that anyone ever asked to leave the squadron.

Our C.O. was Walter Runciman, later Lord Runciman- a brilliant man, a Greek scholar, and way ahead of anyone in the squadron as far as brains were concerned. He had his own aircraft and landing ground up at Doxford, (Chathill, Northumberland). As C.O. he was first class, very steady, and you never had any doubt that he would get you there.

When the war started, he was seconded to the Admiralty. He was put in charge of victualling ships for convoy; he said it was an absolute waste, and the sort of job he had paid a clerk to do before the war.

I was Flight Lieutenant when the war started. At the beginning, we were terribly depressed that we didn't have any really good aircraft. There was a shortage of every kind of equipment at that stage. Anyway, we were sent to Acklington to cover the area between the Firth of Forth down to the Tees, which for one squadron, was quite a large area to cover.

Quite early on, a German plane was spotted patrolling up the coast. It was just having a look around, a reconnoitre. Well, one of our lot who was a barrister in civil life, managed to shoot him down.

The extraordinary thing about this story is that it illustrates just how good German Intelligence was, what extensive files they kept on each of us individually, even at that stage. For when the German pilot was picked up - and he was clearly a highly educated man who spoke perfect English - he said, "To be shot down by a bloody bi-plane, by a bloody barrister, is more than I can bloody well bear."

The Germans were very well briefed. They knew a heck of a lot about us all. I was to experience their interrogation techniques later on in the war.

The first winter of the war, my own squadron and one other were the only two squadrons left still using bi-planes. Churchill was being bullied by the French that the British Airforce weren't doing their stuff as there were only four squadrons in France. When he was eventually persuaded to send a further two squadrons, he said, "Alright. If I have to send two, I'll send the worst equipped squadrons I've got." They were the two Auxiliary squadrons with bi-planes.

We went, that bitterly cold and snowy winter, to Mereville. Having got there, we were then told that we were not allowed to fly because there were no spare parts for our engines, if something went wrong. Of course, the one thing we wanted to do was fly. But it didn't take long to get round the problem. Whenever an aircraft engine was checked, a plug changed or anything, the aircraft had to be tested afterwards. The only way you could test it, was by flying it. As a result aircraft were being checked constantly and plugs changed frequently.

We were eventually sent to different locations. There were plenty of German aircraft about to be dealt with. After we had been to Le Touquet, where the airport was bombed, we started to fly Hurricanes. By this time, I had been given command of our squadron.

Between 1939 and May 1940, we shot quite a few German aircraft down. No one really knows how many, as no exact records were kept. Undoubtedly, the claims were exaggerated, just as they were in the Battle of Britain later. You can't ever claim to have shot an aircraft down unless you have actually seen it crash. Very often, if you had hit a plane, you didn't see what followed because you were too busy getting on and keeping out of the way of things yourself.. I think that I was credited with shooting down seven planes in France and another five or six in the Battle of Britain.

In early May 1940, we were in Belgium. As we listened to the sound of the guns in the distance, a curious incident occurred. A German motorcyclist appeared out of nowhere and started to circle round and round the aerodrome, obviously trying to take stock of things. But we were absolutely amazed at the spectacle of this lone German who had materialsed from thin air, driving in circles round our aerodrome in broad daylight.

We were not the only ones to feel that there must be some significance to this unusual performance. Shortly afterwards, a group of Belgian Army appeared with orders to immediately destroy the aerodrome. "We're very sorry,"they said, "But we have orders to destroy it now."

The next thing was that the Belgian captain appeared with his demolition squad. We told him that it was impossible for us to take off at night and that we must wait until dawn. His response was, "My orders are to blow this aerodrome up."

So we said, "Look! We've got a whole squadron here. We can't take off tonight and you can't blow the whole squadron up."

A discussion lasting four hours then ensued. Although my French has never been very good, we eventually reached a compromise. It was agreed that the Belgians could plant their bombs all over the aerodrome, providing that they left us just one small, clear lane from which we could take off at dawn. As soon as we had left, they could blow the whole thing.

The next morning, they had left the narrow lane that they had promised, in the middle of an aerodrome that they planted with bombs from end to end. It was certainly an interesting experience, and despite the fact that one or two of the pilots weren't very good at starting the planes, we all got off safely in the end.

The next job was to try and halt the German advance into Arras. Twelve aircraft set out. The road from the East into Arras is a very long, straight road and we could see quite clearly what was happening. We dived down on the German transport advancing down the road. What we had not seen quite so clearly, were the German gun emplacements in the fields on either side, moving along on the advance with them. The result was that three of our twelve aircraft were shot down by these side guns, which wasn't a very good score for beating up a couple of German lorries.

That was our last job before flying home on leave. One month later, the Battle of Britain began.

The aeroplane you always hear about in the Battle of Britain is the Spitfire, because it caught the public's imagination. In fact, the Hurricanes shot down far greater numbers of German aircraft. There were more Hurricane squadrons and more Hurricanes. Hurricanes had the same engines as the Spitfires, but were not quite as fast. The Hurricane was an extremely tough aircraft; if you got a bullet in it, it was far more likely to hold together than a Spitfire. It was the name 'Spitfire', that attracted people, and the fact that it was fast.

Whilst the German army were pushing further and further south in Europe, they didn't bother much with the UK. They carried out occasional attacks on convoys, and we were mainly patrolling the convoys and the coastline.

When the Germans started to attack us in force , they started on the ports, and they bombed the convoys more intensively. Then one of our Bomber Commands went over and bombed Berlin. That got Goering and Hitler hopping mad. Their response was: "Right. London next."

That was their biggest mistake. They weren't very bright really. Hence the night raids, daylight raids, everything concentrated on London.

It wasn't until about July that they suddenly woke up to the fact that all they really had to do was to knock out the main fighter aerodromes along the South Coast. Then they could have done what they liked. They did two days of heavy raids on Biggen Hill, and other aerodromes, and they did almost succeed in putting us out.

But the ground crews were absolutely marvellous and very efficient. There were bomb craters all over the aerodromes but they managed to fill them in almost as soon as they were made. Emergency landing arrangements too, were made with great speed.The Germans could have succeeded if they had not once again turned their attention on London.

In the Battle of Britain, they were not attacking us, we were attacking them. Their targets were on the ground, whereas our job was to get up above them, to get behind them, and shoot them down.

When the Germans realised that this was happening, they started to send over Messerschmitt fighters as escorts to the bombers, and then as soon as we attacked, the Messerschmitts went for us. That undoubtedly made it very difficult for us, but it did not defeat us. What could have defeated us was a concentrated bombing attack on the South Coast . Instead, Hitler persisted with this emotional response to our bombing attack on Berlin, by bombing London, and that was his great mistake.

One of the greatest dangers to planes in wartime were the great barrage balloons floating about everywhere. Probably was many pilots were killed by getting tangled up in these balloons as were ever killed by the Germans.

By the time we started offensive raids on France, I had become Squadron Leader. The system was that perhaps three four - engine Lancaster bombers would go accross to attack a target in Nothern France, like Lille Airport, with two or three fighter squadrons as escort. That worked quite successfully — kept the Germans on their toes.

Bombers could carry large petrol reserves but fighter planes had only 45-50 minutes worth of petrol, so these operations had to be carried out pretty quickly.

I was shot down on one of these daylight raids over France. On this occasion, we had bombed the target and everything was going fine. On that day, I wasn't leading, I was No.2. Well, we were on our way home again when the No 1 decided he wanted to see a bit more action, so we turned round again towards France The Messerschmitt Squadron had plenty of advance warning of our action, and as we were climbing up into the sun, they came down on us. I think that our No 1 was the only one to get back home.

It was the most beautiful day and we were fairly high up when the Messerschmitts spotted us. They chased me down to the ground.I thought I might be able to get out and make a run for it, but every time I tried to get the hood open, I was shot at from behind. Eventually, I managed to force land, with the wheels up.

Back at home, I was reported as "shot down in flames", which greatly upset the family. Of course, this is not what happened, and what did in fact happen, was slightly amusing. I landed on a stretch of land between two canals. I was trying to immobilise my aircraft as best I could - but it's pretty hard to destroy a very strong fighter plane when you haven't got something like a hatchet to hand.

As I was doing this, bullets started to hail round me. When you can hear the crack of the bullet, you're alright, because it's gone past, but even so I thought 'Good God, this is no place for me!"

It was a blazing hot summer's day and I was wearing heavy flying clothes and I was sweating like anything as I set off at a run towards the nearest farm house. All the time I was running, the sound of gunfire continued.

What I didn't know then, but learnt later, was that there had been two German soldiers standing on the far side of each canal, when I had landed on the strip of land between them. They could not see each other, but they could both, obviously, see me. One had taken a shot at me, which had whistled past and nearly hit the German on the other side of the other canal. His response was "Damn this English pilot." and he took a shot accross which nearly hit the first German. This went on for quite a long time apparently; these two Germans blindly shooting at each other.

Gunfire still in the distance, I got to a farmhouse and asked, in my schoolboy French, if they could hide me. They said there was no chance, the place was thick with Germans. But if I could get accross the cornfield into the woods, they would come and pick me up that night.

I got into the cornfield and the Germans were there - instantly. They all fanned out and closed in around me; it was just like beating partridge. It wasn't frightening in any way, because I was just so busy trying to work out what to do, how to get out of it. It was just a job. In the event, the Germans got me and funnily enough, I have a photograph of the Germans. and some of the locals, marching me away.

The usual thing when a Wing Commander was taken prisoner was that he would be invited into the German Officer's Mess for a drink. I was not invited in for a drink. I was told that although I had surrendered, I had taken up arms against the German soldiers on either side of the canal. I had apparently shot at them, which surprised me a bit. I didn't know the true story then.

Anyway, a week later our lot shot down a German Squadron Leader. While he was being interrogated afterwards, he mentioned that a British Wing Commander had been shot down the previous week. "We didn't have him in the Mess," he told them, "Because he shot at some of our soldiers."

So, they asked him, "What day was this?" It turned out that the only Wing Commander to have been shot down that day was myself.

This is how my family learnt that I was still alive.

When I was first taken prisoner, it wasn't a hard time physically,the difficult bit was adjusting mentally.

When you were caught, the rule was that you only gave your name, rank and number. That was a bit silly, because you really had to give your home address if you wanted your family to know where you were. They used the Red Cross form as a means of pressure in interrogation. This form had to be signed if you wanted to receive food parcels, which were pretty essential to survival."If you won't tell us the answer to this question, we won't sign your form." But most people obeyed the rules.

It was obviously much easier for the Germans to interrogate individual pilots , each one of whom they had a file on, than to interrogate the entire naval crew of a ship, or a whole army battalion. They must have managed to get quite a bit out of us. They had microphones in the cells and two pilots together, not knowing this initially, might start talking and comparing their experiences.

There was one fellow who was a bit of a wit, and when he was being interrogated, he thought he might as well have some fun.He implied to the  Germans that he had some secret knowledge.

Naturally, they were straight on to it. So he said, "You Germans don't know what's going to hit you next. There's never been anything like it, and I've seen it. I've seen our new bomber. You don't stand a chance when they put it in action."

So the Germans were all ears. "What is this great new bomber of your's called?"

"The name of the new bomber ," said this chap with pride, "Is the Cross and Blackwell bomber!"

Not long after this, every chap who went through interrogation was told, somewhat to their surprise very often, "Don't worry. We know all about your Cross and Blackwell bomber."

The very first food that I got in camp was a slice of that hard, black, German bread. When I was given it, I thought that the Germans were putting me to the test, or putting one over on me. I said, "This must be a joke. This obviously isn't meant to eat." In fact, later I got to quite like that black bread.

I was never seriously hungry in prison, except for the period we spent in a camp in Poland. All the same, we were on the German food ration for gypsies, the unemployed and the over-age.The ration was based on the quantity of calories which were just enough to keep you alive if you did nothing. You did need food supplements.

We got Red Cross parcels, and if you were very lucky you got one a week, 10lbs of food, sheer luxury. When the Germans wanted to be nasty, or there was an escape, they cut the parcels right out for two or three weeks. If you were sensible, you hoarded up some of your provisions.

Germans are not always as bright as they like to think they are. In some of our parcels, we were getting maps and civilian clothes for escapes, and they couldn't work out how the Hell we were getting them. So they had a conference about it, and for two months, every single parcel was opened and checked. Every tin or packet was opened and the contents were poured altogether into a large basin. Flour, beans, chocolate, everything. There was nothing we could do about it, annoying though it was. But they discovered nothing.

We had a Counter Intelligence System in camp, and Dudley Craig was in charge of that. He managed to produce a lot of information. I shared a room with him and both he and I, and other senior people, had been taught a code which we could use to send messages by letter, if we were captured.

The Germans never had the wit to discover how things were coming in. Once every six months you were allowed a parcel from your family. There were a few men who had no family, so we said "Right,we'll invent a parent for each of you." Through the secret code, we arranged for extra parcels to be sent by these 'parents'.

We knew which parcels to look for, and anyway, the Germans gave us the job of distributing the parcels round the camp. The parcels contained the necessary contraband for escape.

The Germans were also incredibly dim about the rather strange sports equipment we received from time to time. At one point, we were sent about a dozen little peg boards with a set of quoits, a child's game which no self respecting man would want to play. But when we took it to bits, we found maps, money and radio valves inside the pegs

If you were to stand a chance of getting any distance undetected after you had escaped, you had to have the right clothes. The uniform of the men in the Fleet Air Arm was very smart, dark blue and tailored by Gieves. We had some good tailors in the camp who could adapt these uniforms into very presentable suits.

We used to take the red or green cloth covers off hardback books and boil them up and that gave us a dye . This worked quite nicely but the only trouble was that the dye wasn't waterproof. So you were alright until it rained and then if you wore a green dyed cap, you were liable to end up with a green face as well.

We bribed the guards to get us local maps and timetables. Certainly in the RAF camps, we were well organised and disciplined about this approach. Only those on the escape committees were allowed to negotiate with the Germans. That was one of the rules. We had a communal fund of chocolate and cigarettes and a market price was arranged to trade these in for items procured by the German guards. The price was controlled so it never became too high. That way we got maps, timetables and money.

Aidan Crawley, who later became an MP, organised this side of things. He was in charge of Camp Intelligence and managed things very well. German speakers were each appointed a German guard with whom to make friends and in whom they had to take an interest and generally butter up.

At one point, so that prison authorities could be seen to be complying with the Geneva convention, a German officer was put in charge of POW welfare. He was quite a soppy character and he got buttered up no end. He was particularly proud of his camera. Now this was very useful to us because we always needed photographs for forged identity cards, passes and passports. So we sometimes managed to persuade him to take a photograph of a group of us, which we would cut up into single photographs.

Sometimes, we got our families to send us photographs from home – of a football team perhaps – and these photographs could be chopped up. We had some brilliant artists in the camp who could alter photographs to more or less resemble anyone.

We had a bank clerk who was the best forger I have ever seen. He literally spent hours "printing" cards with a small paintbrush. Only once did he make a mistake, and that was on an identity card for Aidan Crawley. This was when Aidan managed to escape successfully and almost got to the Swiss Border, where the guards tended to be a bit cleverer. They spotted that March had been abreviated to Mar. on his card, which is never done in German. Just two letters gave, him away. He was recaptured and brought back to camp. You were practically always returned to the same camp when you were caught.

I should think that out of every three hundred POWs who managed to get out, only one would manage to make it back home. Strangely, that didn't really matter. The whole thing about escaping was the whole process of preparation for it. That was the really interesting thing; the plotting and the planning, the ingenuity and of course, the pleasure of keeping the Germans on their toes. The more guards that were needed in a camp, the more

Germans were kept away from the front.

There were two schools of thought about escaping. The majority, about 70 per cent in the RAF camps, whose inmates were young and mainly unmarried, always had their names down for escaping. The other thirty per cent took the view that escaping was an absolute waste of time. "You're not going to get anyone back."they said, which was of course pretty well true. Their view was that it was far more sensible to play along with the Germans and get as many privileges as we could. The argument was that we should make ourselves fit for life after the war by learning languages, studying for something.

Even so, those who were not interested in escaping did suffer badly every time there was an escape, because privileges were invariably taken away for a time. The drama group would have their hut closed down, there were endless parades and Red Cross parcels were stopped. There were reprisals. The non-escapers would say, "We can't get on with anything because of you bloomin' escapers."

But the escape argument prevailed because it was a rule of the RAF."If you are captured, it is your duty to try and escape." We hammered that in as much as we could. As prisoners, we felt that escaping was the one thing we could do for the war. We couldn't do much, but we could do that and it kept us going.

Our first camp, the interrogation camp, was Gulag Luft, near Cologne.There, we learnt pretty quickly that escape attempts were a waste of time unless one had absolute discipline. No one was in that camp for long as it was a transit camp. But everyone thought that they could escape, that they'd spotted some hole in the wire or some other point of exit. You could be quite certain that someone else had spotted exactly the same hole and then you got the situation where people would arrive at that same hole at the same moment, and start arguing about it.

Then we were sent to one of the castle camps which was virtually escape proof, surrounded by a moat. There were wild boars in this moat. If anyone managed to get down there, and it was a thirty foot drop, either they were going to be attacked by the boars or the boars would make such a racket, that the Germans would know that something was up.

We decided to fix the boars by putting used razor blades in the potatoes , which we threw down into the moat. The boars ate the potatoes and they didn't make the slightest difference to them — no ill effects at all.

This castle had previously been occupied by a German family and upstairs in the attic we found some German uniform. So two German speakers among us appropriated these uniforms and used the opportunity of a visit from the Swiss Commission, accompanied by two German officers, to escape. While the inspection by the Swiss and the Germans was taking place, these two slipped down to the gate , hoping to convince the guard that they were the same officers who had just come in. By chance, the guard had changed and he let them out without questioning them. They just walked out — but they were back in two days.

Later on, we got properly organised. The beauty of most escape plans was that they took a lot of organising and occupied a large number of people fairly intensively. Ther whole activity kept your brain working. There would be thirty to forty men sharing the construction of the tunnel but in addition to that, their clothes, passes and all the equipment they would need, had to be prepared by those most skilled at these tasks.

One of the most extraordinary escapes of all was the Wooden Horse Escape, and that was a succesful one. There is a film based on the story, and two books.

The idea of the Wooden Horse was thought up by the very last men in the camp who you would have expected to come up with such a brilliant scheme. These two men had never shown any interest in escaping and neither had they been known to help anyone else in the activity. They were not a particularly popular pair.

Then they astonished all of us on the Escape Committee by presenting us with this exceptional plan. The idea was to make a full size wooden vaulting horse, hollow on the inside, and place it near the wire. Inside, would be the tunnel entrance.Outside, the rest of us would pass our time jumping over this wretched thing.

The problem was that we knew all the men in the camp who would work and put themselves out, and these two men did not immediately fall into that category. At the same time, the rule was that any new escape plan had to be tried. So we had to give it a chance. We thought about it and decided that if we gave them the job of making the Wooden Horse, that would put them to the test.

They had the brains to approach a Wing Commander who was very clever with his hands. He had already made a clock, entirely out of wood, which worked. He was delighted to take on the job of the Wooden Horse.

The whole plan got underway and for a time, things went extremely well. Then what we had feared might happen, did happen. At this point, we had got very nearly to the wire with the tunnel. However, these two chaps would not help out themselves. They wouldn't help dispose of the soil and they expected clothes to be made for them, and papers, and money provided. As the Escape Committee had all these facilities, we laid it all on, that was fair enough. It was really a question of attitude. Eventually, everybody felt that they had had enough of these two and the manner in which they seemed to treat everyone who was working on their behalf.

They literally said, "We're not going to do any more on this. We would do it for anyone else, but not these two. They can stuff it."

For about ten days there was in impasse. Nothing was done at all. The camp had gone on strike. So we said to these two, "OK, find your own team."

But the Wooden Horse plan was far to good to waste. We had to find a way round the problem.

Well, there was an Escape Officer called Oliver Philpotts who had never been out, but who had worked like blazes for other people's escapes. He was well liked , and we felt that if perhaps he could be included in the plan, it would motivate the team to work again.

So we put it to the two chaps that Phillpots should be included in the escape. Initially, they said No. They didn't want that. After some discussion, they were persuaded. The whole camp then rallied round  and the plan took on a new complexion.

So there we were again, endlessly jumping over this bloomin' horse. The Germans were frightfully impressed that we were suddenly so interested in our physical welfare, instead of apparently lounging about.

Eventually the day came when all was ready. The tunnel was completed and they were all beautifully kitted out with clothes, money, passport and papers. Everything. The escape took place, and it was successful for all three of them.

The next thing for us was to delay the knowledge of their escape for as long as possible. The next morning, at roll call, we managed to disguise the fact that three people were missing.

The next day, at morning roll call, we found various ways of disguising the fact that three people were missing. We had a dummy in uniform which we managed to include in one of the rows of men. Then we had rather a small chap who managed to crawl out of his row, having been counted, and stood up with another row, where he was counted again. Even after they spotted the hole, we managed to keep the Germans confused for most of the morning. Morale was very high. We were so elated that we could not stop laughing at the Germans, and they became very cross! At midday, the Gestapo were called in. Twenty of them headed straight for the hut were the camp radio was concealed  inside a table.

Now there was a first class chap in charge of security of the radio. He was also very well in with the Germans. He responded instantly to the situation. He marched smartly up to the Germans, saluted, and said " Herr Kommandant. It is absolutely wrong that your officers should be standing around with papers in their hands. I will get you a table and chairs."

He whistled up four chaps at the double, marched them smartly into the hut, picked up the table and four chairs, carried them out and set them before the commandant. The amazing thing was that it worked. Inside, there were the Gestapo hunting for the radio. Outside, there were the Germans sitting round the radio table and checking through documents on it.

The great thing was to get one over the enemy . On this occasion, we certainly achieved that.

The German rule was, that if one to three people escaped, the alarm was only local. If three to ten escaped, the alarm extended for fifty miles. More than that, and it was a nation-wide search.

In the next door camp, Roger Bushell of "The Great Escape", was in charge of escape operations. They planned this large scale escape. They dug about three tunnels simultaneously, having taken the view that one of them would be discovered. In the event, they got fifty four people out.

At this point in the war, as it was nearing its end, Germany had been very badly bombed and the Germans were in an angry mood. For the first and only time, there was a serious reprisal.They caught just about every one of those men. Then they shot them.

We were shattered when we heard the news. From that moment, escaping was no longer a fun game. All escape attempts were stopped.

As the war drew to a close, we were marched to Hamburg - a week's walk. To start with, the Germans were in complete control. They shot one chap who tried to make a run for it over the fields.But after about three days, we managed to drum it into them that for them, the war was over and it was in their interests to treat us properly. We managed to devise a certificate which, we told them, we could issue for their protection. But we said "Any trouble from you, and we'll see to it that you're shot."Most of them realised that they had lost the war and that it would be better to comply with us. By the time we got to Hamburg, the situation had reversed and we had their guns, and we had them doing exactly as we wanted.

At the end of the war, we were lucky, we were all quite fit.We had had a better time than many. We were young, energetic, enthusiastic. I was married but the majority of the men that I was with, were not.

I would say that one year in POW camp would do nearly everybody good. It made you look after yourself, wash and mend your clothes, feed yourself and not to be fussy about food. It taught you to make the most of what you'd got.

For two years , most people could probably hold their own in those circumstances. If you had a ruling passion, whether it was escaping or a subject you wanted to study - or drama - if you had something you were keen on, you lasted. The drama group put on a new play every two months or so. That kept them quite sane.

A few people gave up. One chap never ever moved from his bunk. He lay there reading or thinking. He used to say, "I'm not giving up, I'm just waiting." One or two people virtually committed suicide by going for the wire and getting shot. One didn't know whether it was home troubles as much as life in prison.

When the war ended, I came home to my wife and son. I had never seen my son , so that was our first meeting. He still talks about the moment when I first walked in and met him; a small boy sitting up in bed at home.

MISS IRENE LAWS

Conscription of women was introduced late in 1941. Women were
conscripted not to the armed forces alone, but for "war-work",
which included the Women's Land Army. Irene Laws was in a
protected profession and need not have joined up, but she
exchanged her office job for service in the forestry section of
the Women's Land Army, the Timber Corps. Her account of her
experiences, reveals the demanding nature of the work - heavy
and dirty toil outdoors in all weathers, yet requiring
considerable skill. She also reveals the inferior conditions of
the service of women who were doing as useful and probably more
arduous jobs as some of those in the armed services. Miss Laws
points to the benefits of her experience, the sense of
independence gained and the friendships formed.

MISS IRENE LAWS

My friend Eileen and I were both in the forestry section of the Women's Land Army, which later became known as the Timber Corps. To start with, people used to assume we were all doing farm work and you sometimes got teased by the locals when they saw you in your dirty dungarees. "Have you finished milking the cows and mucking the pigs out?" It used to get up your nose a bit, when all day long you'd been heaving these tree trunks and pit props around.

I didn't actually need to do this work because I had been working in the office of a transport company and in fact, this was a form of protected employment, so I could have been exempt from war work if I had wanted. I joined up at the time of the Battle of the Atlantic because I felt at that point I wanted to do something to help the country and I didn't feel that I was doing that sitting in an office.

My first introduction to forestry work was in the Carlisle area, in a small wood near Kirk Andrews. I was billeted in a village called Grinsdale. When I first arrived for training, I wondered what I had let myself in for. The wood had previously been on fire and the trees were all blackened. By the end of the day we looked like a lot of chimney sweeps.

By the end of the first week I was suffering from badly blistered heels, insect bites and sunburn.

Then we were sent to Chopwell to train as tractor drivers and it was there I met my friend Eileen. We were trained by Johnnie Ridley, an ex miner, who looked after us like a father. He was always cheerful and he loved to sing. We spent many a happy hour driving along having a sing song.

Tractors are very noisy things, and as the names Irene and Eileen are similar, whenever he shouted for us, it was hard to hear which name he'd called. Either we both rushed over or we both ignored him thinking he wanted the other one. He got so annoyed with this that he gave us each a new name so there would be no confusion. Eileen was known as Jackie and I was called Sammy, and that name stuck with me all through my time in the Timber Corps.

It was very tricky driving tractors over ground covered in tree stumps, dragging logs behind us. If the logs caught the stumps, they could swing in any direction. If we were taking a trailer load of timber to the railway station, we had to remember that the trailer was wider than the tractor. The first time I did this, the trailer caught a lamp post at the side of the road, so I learned the lesson the hard way. Then going uphill on an overloaded trailer, the tractor would rear up on its back wheels so one of us would have to go round and sit on the bonnet to help keep the front wheels on the ground.

When I was sent up to Chathill to work, we also had this great Shire horse which dragged the timber. It was called Bobby and this girl Barbara was in charge of him. When Bobby stumbled against a tree trunk, it amused me the way she used to yell at him, quite cheerfully, "Bobby, lift your bloody dainty feet!"

The work was heavy, and you had to have eyes in the back of your head to watch that the tree trunks that you were dragging didn't get caught in the tree stumps. It was also very dirty work. But I must admit that I enjoyed it most of the time.

The worst time was in the winter when you were numb with cold. If it was wet, the mud was so bad at times, that when you stepped down from the tractor, and then you tried to step back up again, you coudln't. The mud was holding you down. So what you had to do was climb out of your boots on to the tractor, and then heave the boots out of this great soup of mud. It had been even worse before we got our gumboots. At the beginning, rubber just wasn't available, so you wore leather boots with canvas gaiters, and sometimes you were ankle deep in water.

You just got used to it all. You didn't think anything of it after a bit. I suppose when you're young, you just take things in your stride. I certainly wouldn't like to do it now. What the job did teach you was a sense of responsibilty, and it also gave you a feeling of freedom. You were given challenges that you'd never had before. It was quite exciting, for example, driving all over the place on roads without signposts, because they were taken down in the war to confuse the Germans if they invaded.

One of the hardest things was finding billets.

Another friend, Nora, was sent to Kent and she was in a place that had accomodated army camps and army wives and girlfriends. They were fed up with providing lodgings for people . Her landlady told her that she much preferred the men to the girls as they were far less trouble. But once she settled in she was treated very well, as part of the family.

As she was in the country, her landlady kept a good store cupboard and she was well fed, with fresh food every day.

The forces were better catered for in food terms; they had better rations. We were dependent on ordinary people with ordinary rations. For our working day food, the standard fare was paste sandwiches, or cheese and sometimes potted meat. We did get sick of those paste sandwiches. But we found a way of improving them. When we were burning brushwood in the forests, it used to leave this nice hot ash and we used to get a forked stick and toast the sandwiches - smokey paste sandwiches tasted a lot better.

We used to go out on the lorry to work at 7 am and we never got a hot drink until we came back at night time. There were no canteens or anything out in the wild. We got a permit for a thermos flask, an alarm clock, and one or two other things. But the thermos flask always got broken, jumping in and out of the lorries, off a high tailboard. So you ended up with a little bottle like the miners used to have. You used to fill it with tea in the morning, but it quickly got cold. But we put the bottles in the burning ash as well, to warm up the tea. By the end of the day it tasted horrible.

Of course, being in a billet wasn't always easy, because it wasn't your house. You had to put up with your landlady's moods, but it was war time and they had their difficulties too. You just had to grin and bear it. We were only nineteen or so, and we loved the dance music and that sort of thing, on the radio. You'd come in from a long day's work and if there was dance music on the radio, the landlady invariably came in and said 'Oh we don't want that on" and switched it straight off. I never yet had the courage to go and switch someone else's radio either on or off. In my billet, I was mainly reduced to listening to the news.

I sometimes went to Home Guard dances in Beadnell, or to the picture house. The film was changed three times a week.

I used to wangle to get home for quite a few weekends, to Newcastle. I used to hitch hike - we all did - it was quite safe in those days. Many a time I came in on an Army lorry, a Brewery lorry, or a coal wagon even. When I first went away to the country I used to love to get out of it and back to the town - Newcastle, chock a block with people. If I stayed at my billet in Seahouses, there wasn't much to do. You couldn't even get on the beaches because they were all barricaded with barbed wire. If I was stuck out there for more than a few weekends in a row, my one ambition was to get back into Newcastle and see a swarm of people on a Saturday morning.

I must admit though, that I got to love the countryside and eventually, when I was up near Berwick, I used to go on the tractor all on my own, to the railway station and various places. You were just there, trundling along, not a soul in sight, and to me that was perfect peace. I learnt to love and appreciate the countryside in a way I probably wouldn't have done otherwise. That area round the Cheviots is still my favourite to this day.

Of course, it wasn't all peace in the countryside. The airforce used to practice machine gunning on Holy Island. They used to tow these old cars over on to the sands that divide the island from the mainland, and use them as targets. Just after the war, I was up there, and I heard this man saying, when he saw all these old machine -gunned cars that were still there. "Oh, I don't think we'd better take the car over there. Look at all those wrecks in the quicksands!"

There was bombing in Newcastle. In fact, there are still underground shelters all over the city. I was working in Stowell Street when they tried to bomb the Tyne Bridge. Nora had two friends killed when the flats near the soapworks (which they bombed) on City Road were hit. You can still see the evidence of the destruction today. They repaired the building, but you can see the difference in the bricks. When bombs dropped nearby, your windows seemed to come in and go out again, with the force of the explosion.

I think we regretted sometimes that we weren't in the Forces, because they enjoyed advantages that we didn't. We weren't allowed into any of the Forces Clubs. I remember once having to ask a soldier to go into the NAAFI canteen to get me a cup of tea. They wouldn't have served me. That was a bit of a niggle that they would only serve the armed forces, not the voluntary forces.

We were paid about £3 a week and we had to pay for our lodgings out of that, about twenty five shillings.

It was a sore point with the Land Army that we didn't get a gratuity after the war was over. You were allowed to keep your Land Army overcoat, your shoes and two shirts and they gave you twenty clothing coupons. That's what you got for your four year's service; twenty clothing coupons and part of your uniform.

But on the whole, I learned a good deal from my experiences in the Timber Corps, and I got a lot of enjoyment out of it.
It gave me a kind of independence. The other thing was that we had plenty of laughs and most of us formed friendships that have proved to be lifelong. My friend Nora Ratcliffe from Westerhope was also in the Timber Corps and she has helped to bring some of the memories back. Now, she and I both have older members of our families to look after, but we still manage to go away on holiday together sometimes, and enjoy ourselves.

ANDREW MILBOURNE.

Andy Milbourne had what anyone would consider one of the worst
wars possible. He began it as a fit seventeen year old, already in
the Army and ended it on his release from P.O.W. camp minus both
arms below the elbow, and without one of his eyes. A member of the
Parachute Regiment, he had fought in North Africa and Italy
before sustaining his terrible injuries at Arnhem. Operated
on in a primitive and brutal manner and then packed off to Stalag
11B in a cattle truck, the rest of his war was to be spent in the
most appalling conditions. His indomitable spirit is testified
not only by his courage during the war but by his post war
career: as a miner working underground with artificial arms, and
eventually as a Senior Executive Officer in the War Pensions
Office. As so often seems the case, those who have the right to
feel bitter feel little bitterness. Andy Milbourne looks back on
his war with none.

ANDREW MILBOURNE.

I'd always wanted to go into the army, ever since going to camp
with the 17th Territorial Battalion as a boy. But my father, who
was a miner, was dead against it because he was very, very bitter
about the first war. After leaving school, I got a job I didn't
like, working for Hardy Brothers Fishing Tackle. I still yammered
on about the army and I got many a good hiding for it from my
father. In the end, in desperation, he marched me by the ear to
the Drill Hall in Alnwick, where we lived, and presented me to
the R.S.M. saying, "Here's some cannon fodder for you."

When war broke out in 1939, I was just short of seventeen years
old and still doing what you called Boy Service, in Dover. On 3rd
September, we set off for Fenham Barracks and at 11 am when
Chamberlain was broadcasting the declaration of war on
Germany, I got separated from the main body of our group. I got
caught up in the crowds of evacuees moving accross London on the
tube, from Victoria to Kings Cross. Then the sirens went and
there was panic. I finally got Kings Cross and the band master
was in one Hell of a state because he had lost one of his flock.

We came up here to Fenham where I did my machine gun training,
and by June 1940 I had reached the age of man service and I was
posted to Scotland with Commando Operations, but all the time I
was wanting to get into the First Battalion Northumberland
Fusiliers, and get into the thick of things. I was sent to
Armagh, and we were drafted to join the First Battalion in Libya.
We got as far as Portadown before news came that we had been
recalled.

Back at camp, feeling annoyed and frustrated and having had a
row with the RSM, I saw a poster in the Corporal's Mess asking
for volunteers for the newly formed Parachute Regiment, or Royal
Air Corps as it was known then. I filled in the form there and
then and to my great surprise, was called to Belfast at very
short notice, put through various tests, and was accepted.

The commando experience stood me in good stead and I got through
my parachute training quite easily.

Within three months I was on a boat from Liverpool to Algiers,
where I joined the First Battalion for the end of that campaign.
From there I went to Sicily and into Itlaly, then back to North
Africa. After the war, I wrote a novel incorporating my North

African and Italian wartime experiences, but as it was published on the same day as Lady Chatterley's Lover, it didn't get much publicity.

By the time I came home, D Day was imminent. So there was more training. D Day dawned and we were briefed to drop at a place called Evercy. But we didn't go. In fact, we were briefed for a total of 16 different drops (or Ops as they were known) between D Day and Arnhem, and every time the plan changed. It built up a good deal of nervous tension, and we started to lay bets as to whether or not we would drop and, by the time the 17th briefing came, for Arnhem, these bets had cost me quite a bit.

By this stage, we had already been briefed twice for Arnhem. If we had gone after the first briefing, on 3rd September 1944, we would have successfully taken the bridge, held it, and the Second Army would have got through. But they postponed it until 17th September and we were dropped in three lifts. This was unfortunate, because after the first drop, the element of surprise has gone.

Jerry was ready for the Second and Fourth Brigades coming in on the Monday after us. We had dropped on the Sunday, quite unopposed.

Now tea is the most important thing to the British Tommy and I was responsible for our tea rations. The very first question I was asked on arriving at the Battalion R.V. (Rendevous) after dropping, was, "Got the tea Geordie?"

To my dismay and undying shame, I remembered that in my hurried departure from the dropping zone, and my chute, I had left my respirator haversack lying crammed full with tea and sugar. My comrades listened to my confession and with one accord, they shouted: "Bloody Well go and get it then!"

I turned and retraced my steps but hadn't gone far when a burst of machine gun fire made me dive for cover, as hot lead raised spouts in the earth around me. I swore that if I got away from those deadly bullets, I would never drink tea again. After what seemed an eternity, while I'd worked out that I was doomed to lie there, or was almost certain to be cut in half if I ran for it, another burst of fire was suddenly answered from my left.

Without further thought, I made a mad rush back to the RV, and I got there unscathed.

But from about 4.30 that day, the scene changed.

We were advancing towards the bridge to capture a small station in the area of Oosterbeek, about three miles from Arnhem. It was then that we started to come under serious attack from machine gun fire and shelling.

I can remember crawling twenty yards at one stage, towards my selected position. That doesn't sound far, but with hours of intense fighting already behind me, I was cursing the grenades and implements of war hanging from my belt which were digging into my flesh. Sweat was pouring down my face as I was also dragging a 56lb gun tripod behind me. I was No 1, carrying the tripod; No 2 followed behind carrying the gun; No 3 carried the ammunition. That was the team.

Three days later, after fairly relentless and fierce action, in which many of us had been wounded or killed, I was hit by an 88, and My No 2 and No 3 were killed.

I was taken to a cellar, where I lay, for how long, I don't know. I know that I floated in and out of consciousness and that there was a smell of decaying flesh around me which made me feel sick. Water was scarce and medicines and pain killers were very hard to come by. I remember a nurse once giving me some sort of soup. And all the time, shell and mortar fire rent the air - windows crashed, ceilings fell in and the whole inferno nearly drove me crazy.

The pain was intense, particularly in my hands which had been bandaged up. Although a doctor saw me and told me that there was nothing wrong with my hands, neither he nor the nurse nor anyone else would let me see them.

After a time I was taken on a stretcher from the cellar to a hospital. As the stretcher bearers carried me up the road, they were sprayed with machine gun fire from the trees, and they fell to the ground for cover. But we got to the hospital where I was laid between clean white sheets and nursed by German speaking nuns. I was the only Englishman in a room full of the German SS we had been fighting against, and I was attended by German SS doctors.

One of these doctors ordered my bandages to be removed. It was not a pretty sight. Then he gave his instructions: "Amputate." and the word sounds much the same in German.

Later I was wheeled on a bumpy and agonising journey over rough ground to another building. After waiting with many other wounded in a tunnel-like corridor, which magnified the sound of moans and groans, I was taken into a huge and brightly lit room, where a pile of bloody legs and arms lay over in a corner. The whole scene turned me sick.

They did what was called a guillotine amputation, two inches beneath each elbow. My arms and hands were in an awful mess by the time this operation took place, and gas gangrene had set in. My amputation was done by a very primitive and brutal method and after the war I had to have two further operations to tidy things up.

The most frightening thing about it was that although I could see that my hands were no longer there, I could still feel them, as if they were their normal size and length; I had very long hands.

The pain at that time was indescribable and I received no morphine or pain killers, even when my dressings were changed by SS doctors, who often just dragged off the dressings without any preliminaries. It was an example of German ruthlessness that they could treat their own men in the same way. They applied the same technique to the bandages of a very badly burnt German soldier opposite me. He screamed dreadfully and they started admonishing him and pointing to me. After several minutes of this, they slapped him across the face. Evidently it was bad form for a German soldier to scream infront of an English one.

One of my immediate anxieties then, and when I arrived home many months later, was how my parents, particularly my very loving and over protective mother, would cope with their son in this armless condition. At that point I couldn't bring myself to tell them what had happened and I got someone to write home and explain that I had hurt my right hand which was in plaster.

Eventually, I started to pick up a bit and it was suggested that I should be transferred to what had been the Queen Juliana

Hospital, renamed the Alga Meiner, which means General in German.In this hospital, they would fit me with an artifical eye, as I was also minus an eye after Arnhem, and had a broken jaw into the bargain.

But - Oh - that didn't happen. Instead, despite pleas from the nuns, I was taken down to the railway station and pushed into a lousy, filthy cattle truck that was part of a train running back and forth from the Russian front. I was thrown onto a pile of straw, along with a hunk of bread which I had to eat like an animal having no way of eating without assistance. Then someone started to help me. You know how we all helped each other in any way that we could.

It was November and very cold and all I had on was a pair of Red Cross pyjamas. We got to Bremen where there was a terrific air raid going on; bombing by day and by night. The German Red Cross came and gave us some soup, the first meal of the journey.

At Nijkerk, we were ordered off the train with the usual shouting and pushing to get into line - chaps with legs off had no crutches so with much hopping and jumping we started to form up. Then the inevitable counting started; never once, on any parade where Jerry counted us, did I ever see him get it right first go. They are the world's worst counters, but on this occasion their counting was brought to an abrupt halt, as out of the sky, dived one of our Typhoons. End of train journey.

We eventually arrived at our destination, Stalag 11B, a prison camp full of starving Russians who were dying like flies. Typhus had broken out. For food, we were lucky if we got a bowl of skilly (cabbage water) per day, plus four slices of black bread. Infact, cannibalism had broken out, people were so hungry.

They were throwing the dead into lime pits, like something out of Belsen. When any food parcels arrived, the Germans immediately bayoneted the tins so that escape committees couldn't store any food up.

I was at Stalag B for Christmas 1944. For our Christmas celebration, five of us with missing limbs decided to raid some of the Commandant's angora rabbits. My job was to lie near the wire and whistle the tune Lily Marlene if a guard appeared.

But when a guard did approach, I suddenly found that I couldn't purse my lips into a whistle because of my broken jaw. Never mind, we still managed to get hold of some of these rabbits and - Well - the way we ate them - you've never seen anything like it. We were starving men and we had no means of cooking them properly.

The next morning, the Commandant came down to wish us a Merry Christmas. On his way out he turned round and said in his perfect BBC English: "By the way, gentlemen. Someone rather stupidly broke in and stole some of my rabbits. But I am not going to take any action. I don't have to. Very soon I will have some corpses on my hands, so I will know the culprits. I have been keeping those rabbits for experimental purposes.

Well, there was panic. Then this old Northumberland Fusilier who had been badly wounded in the desert, took command. He said "The first one of you to report sick - I'll kill 'em."

Somehow this old Fusilier had managed to hide on his person for a long time, one of those old short bayonets. That was enough for us. Order was restored. Nobody reported sick. At least not then they didn't.

One happy memory I have got of Stalag B was my Birthday in December '44. It was the best Birthday I have ever had. Despite serious shortages of everything, my pal Ginger somehow managed to make me an iced Birthday cake, inscribed "HAPPY BIRTHDAY ANDY, DECEMBER 15th 1944, STALAG X1B." The party was rounded off with one cigarette each.

That was the thing that kept you going, the comradeship, your pals. Some of them I will never forget and there were others, just as good, whose names I'm hard pushed to remember now.

I don't resent or dislike the Germans, but I detested Nazism, Fascism. In the same way today, I hate Communism.

I left Stalag B when I developed nasal diptheria. I was transferred to Obermansfelt , which by comparison, was a Five Star Hotel. I was treated by an Australian POW doctor there. Red Cross parcels came in, supplying us with food and clothing.

When I was dropped at Arnhem, I weighed eleven stone. When I
retruned home to my family in Alnwick at the end of the war, I
weighed six and three quarter stone. It was then, in a way, that
my real battle began, my rehabilitation back into ordinary life.
My career in the army, in the service I loved, was finished. I
had to make a completely fresh start. It was a very difficult
time, not only for myself, but for my family and what I put them
through while I was coming to terms with things!

Looking back now, after retiring from my job as Senior Executive
Officer in the War Pensions Office - a job I really loved and in
which I got tremendous satisfaction from helping people - I feel
that I have been very, very fortunate. Whatever troubles and
heartbreaks may have been my lot sometimes, my beliefs are firm:
faith in God, and faith in my fellow man.

TIMOTHY NORTON

A wartime childhood may include unusual incidents but it can be as happy and secure as any peacetime childhood as long as one essential element is supplied - family love. Timmy Norton's early years in a country house in the village of Whalton were more comfortable and secure than those of many war-time children; but he shared with those whose fathers were in the services, and especially those whose fathers, like his own, were POWs, the experience of having to get to know a stranger, who was his father, at the war's end. This is a vivid, amusing and affectionate evocation of a child's world, with a rather larger cast of characters than most: a big family because countless female relations came to stay for the duration of the war, and their numbers were equalled almost by the number of servants in the household. Some aspects of life continue as pre-war. There are no food shortages in the menage - but then all classes in the countryside did better in this respect than their urban counterparts - and some petrol is usually available. But a wing of the house is taken over by the army, the laundry becomes the Home Guard H.Q. while the village mobilises at the sound of a drunken farmer's noisy homecoming.

TIMOTHY NORTON.

I was nought when the war started, and I was born in 1940. My father was captured by the Germans in Crete and his account of his internment is quoted in the two histories of his regiment, The Northumberland Hussars. Those captured on Crete were kept in squalid and inhumane conditions to start with and my father's description makes grim reading. Naturally, I was not aware of any of this as a very small boy living in a large and very well ordered household. My mother must have been continuously preoccupied about my father, but perhaps there were so many of us at home, I don't remember being affected by any atmosphere of prevailing worry. Although, my family were in shipping and a sense of anxiety did filter through about that. That was a fairly constant worry and we did lose some ships in the war, three I think.

My father was a prisoner until the end of the war and he did not see me until I was five years old. He always said that the best thing about being imprisoned by the Germans was that he didn't have to see me until I was five - a merciful relief quite frankly!

When the war started, my mother moved here, to Whalton, from the Old Rectory in Ponteland where she and my father started their married life. At that time, this house belonged to my mother's parents. My grandfather definitely thought that if the Germans invaded, he would call the whole family here. He had even made a plan, in the event of German occupation of Whalton, for us all to evacuate to three fields away to one of our farms, the North Farm, where the farmer was under instructions to have a twelve bore gun permenantly at the ready.

My grandfather had millions of female relations, no men at all, and no sons. Whether my grandfather had invited them or not, all these females turned up here to live for the duration of the war. There were aunts and cousins as well as my mother and sister. My Great Aunt Min, my grandfather's sister, who was a widow, was among them. She was a very wealthy lady. She did aboslutely flog all; she wouldn't even put a log on the fire. Her husband had actually been chairman of Newcastle Breweries. She brought her Rolls Royce with her, which was laid up in the garage.

We all had nannies and my sister and I had a Nanny each. There were housemaids, nurserymaids and a cook. There were Goodness knows how many women. The nannies looked after us and my mother and grandmother looked after the nannies and the nursemaids, and sorted out their squabbles. I remember one dreaded nursemaid, who after a row with me, put my teddy bear through the washing mangle to spite me. I have still got the bear.

The laundry was the Whalton Home Guard's headquarters, stacked up with steel hats and gas masks. The gas masks are still there.

Our cook always wore a white coat and was very bad tempered. She used to sharpen the kitchen knives on the stone window sill outside. When she was in a particularly bad temper, she used to take Hell out of that window sill with her knives; you can still see the marks. But she did make these marvelous Chelsea buns. Nobody ever discovered her recipe for these exceptionally good buns. It died with her.

There was a gardener and a joiner and a chauffeur, Raper. The most marvelous man as far as I was concerned was our butler, Burton, who was with my family for forty years. He was a great ally to me. When the nannies squabbled amongst themselves about what the children got to eat, Burton always saw to it that when we got chicken, I got the breast and the girls bloody well got the legs.

There had been nothing but girls in my family for ever and ever, and an awful thing to say is that I must have been monumentally spoilt. Luckily, I don't remember being aware of it. Although it has to be said that when I was born, they did hang the Union Jack and any flags they could find, out of the front window.

Burton did absolutely everything. Everybody dreaded Thursday, which was his day off. Every morning he put on his apron and cleaned the silver in the pantry, laying out the forks in rows. Every single morning he did this, and ofcourse, it wasn't necessary. Then every single night of the war, Burton put on a white tie to serve dinner. Meals were still very formal. Burton was too old for war service, but he had been in the first war, where he had developed trench foot from which he suffered for the rest of his life.

He was in the village home guard, and one night at dinner there was suddenly the sound of some awful noise building up in the distance. The noise got louder and louder and seemed to be coming nearer and nearer. Well, the Balloon went up so to speak. The whole ARP force came out to Whalton's defence, including Burton who had to drop his silver salver in the middle of dinner and put his tin helmet on, and probably still wearing his white tie, he set off for the village - all men to the ready!

It was shortly discovered that the cause of this appalling noise was a farmer, completely pissed, returning home in his car and oblivious of the fact that his steel wheel cover was half off and was banging against the car as he careered along the road, making a Hell of a racket.

We occupied the whole house until the west wing was requisitioned for soldiers. We didn't see much of them. There was a very strict division between their billet in the west wing and the private side of the house. My grandmother used to rocket them the whole time over their dustbins. Infact I met one of the soldiers who had been billeted here just the other day, and he told me that he had been terrified of my grandmother.

I was very fond of my grandmother. She was also nice to me; a very good egg. At that time, I can remember her permenantly doing up parcels. She was always sending those egg boxes full of rations, to relations who weren't here. I think that my mother was included in this task. Certainly she must have sent parcels to my father. I think that she did some other kind of war work, but I forget what. My mother is a very capable person, but there is one thing she cannot do and that is cook. She once made a cake using umpteen eggs; it turned out black and rock solid.

My grandmother got so much into the habit of wrapping up brown paper parcels that she continued to do so even when the war was over. I got so many food parcels when I was at Eton that I didn't always get around to opening them. One day, my mother came to see me at school and discovered a pile of rancid butter parcels in my cupboard. It was that deep yellow butter you get from Jersey cows, but there weren't any preservatives in it. My grandmother was once accused of colouring her butter at the village show.

She was mortified and never displayed her butter there again.

Food was rationed, but because of our farm we were very fortunate. Another crisis was fuel. The boiler here was fired by coke. There was no central heating in this house. I can't remember any heating in the nursery wing, where we children were. It was fairly spartan. There was one miserable one-bar fire, which Nanny used to sit almost on top of. The night nursery was north-facing and absolutely arctic.

Petrol was very restricted, but my grandfather, who suffered from Parkinson's Disease, but still went to business in Newcastle, got a bit extra. Raper the chauffeur drove him.

My mother's sister, who also lived with us, (and her daughter), had had a sad time as her husband, a doctor of such brilliance that he was near to madness, committed suicide. So in part to keep herself occupied, she spent a certain amount of time doing war work in London. But she was very much a get up and go person. She has been married three times since then.

She was quite a tomboy, and when she came here, she was banned from going anywhere in the car by my grandfather. Raper the Chauffeur used to take the keys out of the car when she was at home. But we had an estate lorry here and one weekend, my aunt was invited to some party in Newcastle, and she discovered that the keys hadn't been removed from the lorry. So she set off to the party in that, which caused a rumpus. I think she gave my grandparents a Hell of a time. She was extremely naughty and very flighty, but enormous fun. Her daughter, my cousin Pam, loved it here, and really always thought of this house as her home.

Everything here was terribly well ordered. Perfection really. There was always someone to make sure that I never lost my hankie or my cap. This was my war.

We had a governess too, who for some reason we nick-named the Queen of Puds. We shared her with the Renwicks and Browne Swinburnes and the Pumphreys. To eke out the petrol, we took it in turns to have the lessons in each of our houses. Wednesdays were always at Capheaton, where we had rabbit for lunch which still had hairs on the legs. The schoolroom here was the ballroom, which was built for dances, but never used for one, and then pulled down. Sometimes we used to go by bus to the other houses, sitting on slatted wooden seats. Mrs Browne- Swinburne used to meet us all at the end of the drive in a little Morris Eight.

The ordered pattern on events was occasionally interrupted by bombs. Stray bombs were sometimes dropped by planes being pursued by one of our fighter planes. One went through a window in Bolam Church, but luckily didn't explode. I do rememember, although it seems exactly the converse of what one might expect, my grandmother taking me up to the roof to watch the bombers flying back from Edinburgh. There was a direct hit on a local farm. Thefarmer came back from the pub one night and thought he had the DTs because all he could see were chickens running around with no feathers on - they had been blown off by the bomb blast. Then he realised, a ten to one chance, that the entire place had been demolished.

When the war ended, everyone was waiting for my father to come back, and my mother was obviously very excited. She didn't know exactly when my father would be brought home. She received various duff messages and I think that she went to London more than once in expectation of his arrival, and stayed there for a few days. Then he wouldn't be on the anticipated plane, and she would return home, very depressed. Their designated meeting place was the Ritz and eventually all came right; they met up there and later set out on the journey back to Whalton.

My sister and I were all dressed up in our best clothes for my father's homecoming. I can remmber his first appearance as clearly as if it was yesterday. This figure, my father, who I had never met before, walking in through the door there.

The confusing thing for me was that "Daddy" had always meant my grandfather to me, because this was how my mother always addressed my grandfather. My father was always spoken about as Petre. Then this other chap appeared who was Daddy. So for quite a time I called my father "Daddy Petre". He brought me a present, a silver watch which I still have, and a present for my sister. But it was all very mystifying to me, and I was confused for quite a time.

My nose wasn't in the least put out of joint by my father's

arrival. It was simply that I didn't need him, or rather, didn't yet feel that I needed him. Yet it was clear that he had some role in my life. A role that up to that point had been filled by Burton our butler, and the man I had thought of as Daddy, my grandfather. I wasn't used to the idea of a father. Infact, a father to me then, seemed a totally unecessary encumbrance.

I am close to my father now. We get on very well but I am not cosy with him in the way that children are with their parents today. I think that to meet your father for the first time at five years old, as I did after the war, definitely does affect one in some way.

MRS LAVINIA ORDE.


The Field Auxiliary Nursing Yeomanry was born of the Boer War.The
women who volunteered for this most dignified organisation
then found themselves labelled F.A.N.Y.s, an acronym which
inevitably raises a wry smile.
In 1939, this unit was a transport corps striving to maintain
its proud identity and tradition on its incorporation with the
recently founded ATS. Lavinia Orde's war began as a F.A.N.Y.
driver navigating the frozen lanes of southern England in the
winter of 1939-40; the fortunes of war then took her as ATS
officer to North Africa and from thence to the Italian campaign.
She had what is sometimes called a "good war": she was promoted,
handled new responsibilities, made friendships (including that of
a future cabinet minister) and developed new ideas. (She is one
of the few raconteurs to claim that the war moved her to the
left politically, a shift which many historians have argued was a
general tendency in the war years).She loved the army and
military life, but there is nothing conformist in her outlook;
her views are refreshing and often original. Her post-war
marriage to a Northumbrian army officer brought her to
Northumberland, where she has lived ever since.

MRS LAVINIA ORDE.

In 1938, I 'came out' and did the season in a more or less
conventional manner for a year and then I continued into the next
year but things became a little more free, a little less
restricted. During my second season one could be asked to a dance
and on the invitation was written "and Partner". One no longer
had to be chaperoned by one's mother.

However, one was aware of some disturbing developments on the
political horizon and I decided to join the F.A.N.Y.s, an elite
military corps, born in the Boer War, when F.A.N.Y.s in neat blue
and red habits rode side-saddle to pick up the wounded in the
field. By the First World War the F.A.N.Y.s were mechanised and
drove some of the first military vehicles. Their name was changed
officially to Women's Transport Corps, but we were of course
affectionately known by the old name of F.A.N.Y.

I went to summer training camp and was drilled by Guards
sergeants and learnt to drive an army lorry. I gladly missed the
dance of the Season, Sarah Spencer Churchill's dance at Blenheim,
to go to camp. My mother must have been very disappointed but she
never showed it. We had to pay for our officer type uniforms, and
for camp. We were called Troopers, but when the A.T.S. was formed
shortly before the war, we were incorporated as the transport
section, and our rank was changed to Volunteer. But all the same,
we clung to our Sam Brown belts and Yeomanry traditions.

So I was enlisted with the F.A.N.Y.s and was issued with a sealed
envelope of secret orders which I was only allowed to open on
receipt of a telegram from head quarters. The message on the
telegram would be "Radiator Bust !"If you were able to report
within forty eight hours, you had to send a reply telegram saying
"Mended." The minute my telegram came, I rushed upstairs and
changed into my uniform. I opened my orders only to find that my
"secret" destination was a building only a few yards away from my
father's office.

I was called up three days before war broke out. I was paid nine
shillings a week, much of which was spent on chocolate Bath
Oliver biscuits which I used to eat when the officers did not
invite me into their mess for lunch.

It is extraordinary now, to recall the insouciance with which we entered the war. The diary that I began to keep in an army excercise book dutifully presents the arguments for and against pacifism, the new order for Europe, etc. In fact, what we F.A.N.Y.s were really thinking about was which car we were going to drive, which officer we would be driving and whether night duty would interfere with our social life. I do not remember feeling any fear at that stage, or even much later in the war. I am lucky rather than brave in that I have never been worried by the prospect of physical danger.

I don't know what we expected of the war. We just got on with things and did them as we were told to do them. I think perhaps that if we had any expectations, they were heroic ones of going to the front and rescuing a general or something like that and getting a V.C.!

To start with, the staff officers for whom we were driving, were rather terrified of us, because they were not yet used to having us around. I remember once, in the early stages of the war, that I mutinied against two of our own officers and refused, one night, to prepare their dogs' dinners for them. I said "Do them yourselves, Ellis and MacEnzie!" They obediently did so, too wary of us to disagree. In fact, doing the dogs' food had only been a concession and was not part of our official duties, even when we had to take our turn as cooks, for which we were even less fitted than for drivers.

Being an inexperienced driver, I had a few minor accidents and as a punishment was set to drive Hygiene sergeant majors around in Morris Minors. Next, I drove an ambulance for a tiny military hospital in Stow-on-the-Wold. I was billeted with an old lady who made delicious hand-made chocolates. I got my horse over to the village too, and used to clean my boots and bits in the nurses' sitting room until they complained. I transported hay for my horse in the ambulance.

The first winter of the war was a very hard and cold one and we used to get dressed under our bedclothes in the morning. There were some vehicles that we had to drive without windscreens. That was excruciating but we had to put up with it. I am afraid that I have always been rather intolerant with people who are greatly concerned with physical comfort. It is something that has never really mattered to me. Obviously war time helped to confirm that attitude.

I spent two years in the ranks, my university period, my tutors being two officers I drove. They were both Jews, one a T.B. doctor, the other a successful author, Robert Henriques. We used to have wonderful conversations on those long night drives, returning from visiting army units. I used to write up these talks fully in my diary. It was my idea of heaven: Proust, Aldous Huxley, Evelyn Waugh, Koestler, Orwell, Isherwood and Auden, - I read them all, thanks in part to the influence of these two officers.

The T.B. doctor did sometimes ask me up to see his etchings, but I always used to say that I had to get home to clean the car. This was quite true; however late we got back, we had to clean them every night. The standards set were very high but they had to be for good discipline. The army works out everything so that even its simplest minded member can cope. We had sixteen obligatory tasks, checking the car over, that we performed in order whether the car needed it or not.

There was inevitably a lot of waiting about in the car and I used to sit there munching my chocolate Bath Olivers and reading. I also tried to teach myself, not very effectively, shorthand and typing.

I became an L/C driving instructor. I enjoyed it because it involved teaching, something I'm good at. However, I was always in trouble at the training centre for not wearing a hair net and for walking about in a "carefree" manner, and for not cleaning the bottom of my ambulance properly.

In the F.A.N.Y.s, our appearance and the way in which we presented ourselves was regarded as very important. The F.A.N.Y.s were very aware of this because when we merged with the A.T.S., we were determined, by making certain adjustments to our uniform, to show that we were different from the A.T.S. The fact that most people in the F.A.N.Y.s did come from the same social background did have something to do with it. We used to wear lanyards, dipped in coloured ink, on our left shoulders, and our cap straps over the top of our caps instead of round the front in the ordinary manner. These privileges of appearance were something we fought for to the death almost. I mean some people actually left the A.T.S because they were not allowed to enforce these minor measures of distinction.

But the odd bits of trouble and bother I had while I was a driving instructor convinced me that it was essential that I became an officer,so I was sent on a course at the Officers' Training Centre in Edinburgh and after six weeks I got mycommission and was sent to Reigate. I was a very conscientious officer and I remember inspecting billets, and opening the occupants' drawers to find fearful mixtures of mouldering apples and dirty laundry. I also learnt to shoot armed infantry weapons in preparation for the Invasion and I marched happily at the head of my platoon in preparation for victory parades.

After this, I became a military police instructor and was able to teach to my heart's content. I taught an enormous range of fascinating subjects from Military Law and unarmed combat, to outlining the problems of V.D.

By 1944, I had a very definite yearning to go abroad. I must admit that I had enjoyed many aspects of my own minute contribution to the war effort and I was fascinated by life in the army. From my own point of view, the thing about the army was that once you had been in it a year or two, you absolutely understood how to get what you wanted and how to manipulate it to your own advantage. That was why when I left the army after the war, I was lost, for a time, because I had known no other adult life. I had left my cosy little niche in the army I knew so well.

In 1944, I was also feeling very strongly about the suffering in Europe, and had by this time heard about the concentration camps. I went to Staff College for a month and learned about all the German divisions, especially the S.S. ones, which was useful later when I worked at an educational establishment for German P.O.W.s at Wilton Park after the war. I did quite well at Staff College and played the part of a woman commandant welcoming students - I laughed so much at my own jokes that I could scarcely finish the lecture.

I was then sent abroad, destination: North Africa. I was very sad saying goodbye to my parents but at the same time I was terribly excited and tried not to look too much so. From my personal point of view, things became more exciting and more enjoyable from then on. One was aware, in wartime, that one was living through something that one could put one's whole heart and soul into; one was living a completely integrated life in a way in which one seldom could again. There was no dilemma about what one should or should not do, except perhaps just how hard one should work.

We departed on our voyage from a secret embarkation point. Ofcourse, army convoys were being torpedoed day and night, but I don't remember feeling the slightest fear; by that point, we never had the slightest doubt that we were winning.

When we arrived in North Africa, I can remember the excitement of seeing the oranges growing, experiencing the heat, and seeing the sunburnt knees of the 8th Army, the Desert Rats. We were given a pep talk on arrival and told two things: we had to wash all fruit thoroughly before eating it, and we were not to lose our heads as we were so much in the minority as women.

Naturally, relationships were formed, but almost none of the girls that I was with there married until after the war. Marriages had a difficult time in the war. Only a few of those I knew who had married before the war, managed to keep their marriages intact by the end: couples had lived separately through different wartime experiences and had developed in different directions and often found they had few points of contact when they met again.

Next, I was sent to Italy to work as a staff officer in General Alexander's H.Q. I sometimes drove his Daimler and we used to go riding with him and other officers through the vinyards near Casserta. V.E. day came while we were there, but it made little difference to our lives with the thought of the Japanese still to deal with. At the same time, we were entirely selfcentred in our Army group which was dominated by General Alex, whose personal badge we wore on our pockets.

While I was in Italy, two important things happened. The Japs were finished off, and there was a General Election at home. By this time, I was no longer a Conservative. I looked at those whom I had accepted as born to rule and saw them as being no more intelligent, idealistic, hard-working or efficient than members of the working classes. I remembered some of the rich, insensitive , bigotted Conservative M.P.s I had come accross and I changed my political direction to the Left. I think that I had been gradually moving in this direction for some time and the experience of war consolidated my views.

There was another factor that probably did effect my political outlook. While I was in Italy, I became friends with a major in the 8th Army, who later became a most distinguished Labour Party politican and cabinet minister. He was one of the most refreshingly intelligent, down to earth and enthusiastic men I have ever known. After only a few months in Italy, he seemed to know an incredible amount about Italian culture in general, and spoke excellent Italian. He also played the piano, and discovered Opera, as I did, in the land of Verdi, and has since become a great expert.

We met each other at an Italian political meeting. We did quite a lot together including endlessly discussing politics and driving about Umbria singing communist songs with Italian peasants that we picked up in the jeep.

Sadly, our ways parted when the war in Europe ended. He went back to stand for Parliament and I was posted to Vienna in the Control Commission as P.A. to a general. We saw each other again when he came to lecture at the P.O.W camp at Wilton, where I worked after the war.

He was an influence on my life that I valued a lot. He taught me a greater understanding of politics and a deeper respect for politicans. I have always followed his career with interest and occasionally think back to the days when we discussed the beginning of social democracy in Europe.

Despite his and other influences, I still did not feel that I could vote Labour in the General Election. So I voted Liberal. None of my political friends got in, in that election. When Labour won, we nonetheless rejoiced. We felt sorry for Churchill and we felt grateful to him too, but we saw him as a wartime leader and we looked for the changes that we hoped Peace would bring.

I had loved the military life and very much missed the security of it when I was demobilised. When I met my husband, an army officer, in the early nineteen fifties, one of the things that attracted me to him was that he represented the soldierly qualities I so admired; loyalty, lack of fuss, lack of conceit, efficiency and courage, smartness and short hair too. Marrying Peter took me back into the world of the army again.

## MISS MARJORIE PRINGLE

A doctor's or nurse's war experience always makes salutory reading, in that invariably they see little of the excitement of battle, but much of its unpleasant consequences, the wounds without the bugle. Marjorie Pringle's account of her time as a Queen Alexandra Nursing Sister in India and Burma is particularly interesting, both because the war in the Far East added the dangers of cholera, dysentry, malaria and dengue fever to the risk of injury in battle, and because of the light she throws on the more beneficent side-effect of war, developments and improvements in medical techniques. Marjorie Pringle clearly derived enormous satisfaction from her work and she makes little of the heat and discomfort which she must have endured, and the very long hours. Her reminiscences include intriuging glimpses of the last years of British rule in India.

## MISS MARJORIE PRINGLE

The advantage of being a trained nurse was that you didn't have to change your profession; nurses are needed in both war and peace. I trained at the Royal Victoria Infirmary between '37 and '41. I always had itchy feet to travel, and before the war I had thought of joining the Colonial Service, because in those days we still had an Empire at our disposal. Anyhow, I think that anyone who lives on an island tends to get the travel bug at some stage.

We were well into the war by the time that our training ended, and there was a great call for S.R.N. nurses. So we rose to the occasion. We did not have any idea where we would be sent.

In December '41, we were sent down to Netley, Southampton, which had just about been bombed flat. We did not experience the real Blitz in the way that my sister, also a nurse, had in Birmingham. Nonetheless, we had experienced quite enough bombing raids.

We developed real astaying power. We all lived in the hospital in those days, and we worked very long hours, but it was supposed to be a noble profession so you didn't mind. When you are young you have this enormous amount of energy.

Nobody knew what was going to happen next, until one morning someone came into the dormitory where we nurses slept, and poked us awake at about 3 a.m. We were told to get up and prepare for departure. I can remember that we were then issued with a square of corned-beed sandwich each, and then we had to sit at Southampton Station, where we were stuck until seven o'clock that evening.

The train, when it eventually came in, was the longest I have ever seen. We still did not know where we were going and this feeling of uncertainty was not eased by the fact that there was no fluid of any kind on the train. We travelled through the night, and you can imagine what a weary business it all was. That first journey will stay with me for ever.

We arrived at Gourock, on the Clyde at 7 a.m. in a thick mist, but looming through it was a big ship, the Windsor Castle. We boarded the ship and we were told to wear trousers and never to undress, so that we could evacuate the boat at any point if necessary. It was all rather frightening and we still didn't know where we were going; nobody dared to say anything, even if they did know.

It turned out that we were on our way to Singapore. We were in a convoy of about thirty ships, and apparently we were attacked about nine times on the journey, but we never felt it as we were right in the centre of the convoy. The Navy was quite marvellous really.

We never got to Singapore; the Japanese got there first. When Singapore fell it was the most awful thing — we had all thought it was impregnable. Some of my colleagues from the RVI in Singapore were told to leave, and as they were leaving, they were shot on the boat.

We ended up in South Africa instead of Singapore. That was lovely. It always upsets me when I hear criticisms of the South Africans because they were straight down to the boats to greet us, and they couldn't do enough for us. We stayed on the boat awaiting orders, which suited us. The soldiers though, had to do a route march around and as a result, there were a lot of sunstrokes to deal with.

When we got our postings, some troops were sent to Madagascar, and we nurses were sent to India. They didn't really know what to do with us once we got there, but they said we'd have to go right up to the northern end, into Burma. My colleague and I were sent to Faizabad and someone said, "Anywhere with bad on the end is desperate."

We took the train from Bombay early in the morning, and we travelled all day and well into the night. I started to wonder if we would ever get there. So when we drew in at Lucknow, a place which I was quite interested in because I knew about the Siege of Lucknow, I said my colleague, "How's about getting off here and finding a hotel?" The smell of Lucknow was appalling, and the station was covered in people sleeping — every inch of it. We got a rickshaw to a comfortable hotel with mosquito net beds, but we still couldn't sleep for the noise of the crickets.

Faizabad is in the old United Provinces in North India, about eighty miles from Lucknow. We did not have far to go the next morning and, after our night in the hotel, we were able to set off clean and tidy. We never dreamed that people had been sent to meet us at Faizabad at 5 a.m. in the morning, so we found that we were in trouble when we got there! It was not the best of arrivals, as there was a dust storm blowing as well, and the heat was quite awful.

We were taken to the hospital at the old cavalry station there. I was glad that we had been sent there because there was plenty of work to do at that point, because people were walking out of Burma, a big evacuation. In no time at all, the wards were full. There were a lot of Indian patients and the hard thing was, that we had no knowledge of their language. Of course, the patients used to play on this, they were in their element We had a 'Munchi' who tried to teach us Urdu, although I think he was more interested in learning English. We had a dictionary, and understood enough Urdu eventually, to get by.

The next thing, we had a cholera epidemic. It was really hectic. Cholera destroys very fast, so we were going round in circles, administering to them , trying to keep them alive. The patients lay on split paliasses with a pail underneath to catch the liquid loss, and the stench was pretty awful. We had them on intravenous drips to make up the loss of fluid. Later on when I had been transferred to Gauhati, in another cholera epidemic, we had about a hundred cholera victims, and we only lost ten of them, which was pretty good.

To protect us, all the hospital staff were given cholera injections very frequently. Although, I think that women must have a different immune system to men. I got a slight attack of malaria, but I never had a temperature. I am just one of those people who feels rather under the weather for a long time, unwell, but I am never really ill. I did get dengue fever, and I got these very painful eyes which I couldn't move to right nor left without hurting. My friend was laid very low with that; dengue fever is a mixture of rheumatism and malaria. You feel terribly ill and then start getting the itch.

It was unfortunate for us that we had arrived in Faizabad in February, because not long off that, it started to heat up terrifically - it does this before the monsoons in May. When the monsoons start, you just want to go out in the rain in the nude and get completely saturated. By the time the monsoon finishes, you are sick of it, because the damp causes mould to develop everywhere.

After ten months at Faizabad, when I had got aclimatised to the dry heat, I was called to go with the 14th Army.

I packed my bags and took my bicycle with me - at Faizabad, we travelled everywhere by bike. Everyone seemed to do that, as it was very rough ground for walking. The bicycles were awful too, but never mind, they moved.

I travelled by train to Calcutta, in the company of four men and my bike. It was quite wrong that I should have been in a carriage with these men really, against the rules. On the journey we all had to lay down together, but as the rules were so strict, nobody would have dared touch me!

When we arrived in Calcutta, there was a strike. It was a time of great upheaval; there were campaigns to get rid of the British, to end British rule in India. I was only in Calcutta for five days, but looking back on it , I don't think I realised how disturbed and upset I was by the sight of so many dead and dying people, lying around in the gutters, on the streets. There was a rice famine at that point, and as some of the Indians were paid in rice, there was neither pay nor food for them. This was the most awful contrast to the beauty of this great British Raj City. I remember going to the big Army Hospital there - the one that you saw the television production of "The Jewel and the Crown."

From Calcutta it took two days to get to Gauhati, which in the guide book was described as "The seat of culture and learning, the gateway to Assam." That was not quite how I found it°

The hospital was very large; it had been a zoological college. We slept in the cantonment there. There were about fifteen hundred beds in Gauhati, and the patients were British and practically every other nationality you could lay your hands on. Fortunately, the Colonel was a Professor of Tropical Medicine who had been in Singapore, and they had managed to get him out. He was absolutely terrific, and very go-ahead, Colonel Ranson,and he decided that the hospital must have an Intensive Care Unit. He interviewed everybody and he knew two professors from the R.V.I., so I was on his team. There were no nurses there, only sisters and RAMC orderlies, until the Red Cross nurses started to come out.

The Intensive Care Unit needed experienced people, and Colonel Ranson ran it like a teaching hospital. It was absolutely fascinating work, although, in that heat, it was hard going, but you adjust your body and you learn to go at a certain pace. Colonel Ranson used to say, "You must have a whisky at six o'clock every evening " I hated the stuff, but I learned to like it, and it raised your blood sugar level.

The heat was such that the theatre sisters had a terrible time. They had to get up at midnight to work, when the air was at its coolest. Just before we left to go into Burma, Lord Nuffield gave us an air-conditioner,but we never got the benefit of it.

At Gauhati, we got all the wounded from the Battle of Kohima, which I was told was a slaughter. The battle had gone on for weeks and supply lines had been blocked by the Japanese so Kohima was under siege for a long time and many of the wounded were very undernourished as well as everything else. A little before that, Orde Wingate had been carrying out his operation in the Chindit Hills: when he organised his attack on the Japs, he told the men as they went in, that there was no organisation for getting them out. They had to get out any way they could – it was every man for himself. So you can imagine, we got quite a few of the Chindits.

The great improvement that we benefited from at Gauhati, was the use of penecillin. When you got men in from Kohima with potential gas gangrene, the peneçillin worked like a miracle. It was kept on ice, and then you mixed it up, and then you gave it to the patient every three hours exactly. You couldn't give it through a drip or intra-muscular, as we didn't know enough about that then. (The first penecillin, which we had used at the RVI, was Prontosil, which turned your urine pink. Before that, we only had the various sulphur drugs.)

For light relief, there was a certain amount of entertainment organised. There was a chap who was very keen on amateur dramatics, and it's suprising how much talent people have when they are given the chance. So plays were produced, and the troops enjoyed that as much as any of the variety shows put on by ENSA.Wendy Hillier and Peggy Ashcroft came out, but independantly of ENSA. Noel Coward came out too, but he took an awful lot of looking after!

When I got my leave, I sometimes went up to this lovely hill station called Shalong, where you could smell the pine trees, and it was much cooler. There were some lucky bods who were stationed there, but I actually preferred to work where I was in the thick of it. I got to the point at Gauhati where I started to feel that being there was my whole life. After all, by the time I left Gauhati, I had been away from home for nearly four years.

During our time in India, we had all got used to dealing with people who were very, very ill. We had nursed typhoid, cerebral malaria, black water fever and two cholera epidemics. We also all had dysentry ourselves - everyone - you couldn't help but get it.

After D Day, the whole caboodle, the medical staff, packed up and moved to Chittagong. That was terrible. There were dreadful floods and we lost a lot of equipment. Also, to my lasting regret, I lost my five year diary which I had kept every single day throughout the war. At Chittagong, we were only in transit, waiting to get mobilised. After two weeks, they sent us to Rangoon.

Rangoon was the most magnificent city which had been laid low. They had to spray the whole place with DDT - everything was polluted and filthy, dogs running wild all over the place.

We were based in a big university building constructed round a large quadrangle. First of all it had to be cleaned, scrubbed out, and we all had to get in, and get down to it. We were preparing for what was to come after the final push.

On the last onslaught against the Japs, the troops had to go into the Jungle during the monsoons. It was an offence for any soldier not to take this prophylactic, Neprocrine, which gradually turned you yellow, but was a protection against malaria. We were always having to check the medical supplies, as there were a number of Indians in Rangoon and some worked at the hospital, and given half a chance, they took the drugs and sold them - replacing them with something like soda bicarbonate tablets. They were terrible! You had to count every tablet, keep everything under lock and key.

The war brought tremendous advances in medicine. For example, at the RVI before the war, doing a blood transfusion had been a tremendous performance, often done from person to person, direct. When we started blood transfusion units in the war, that was the beginning of storing blood. It didn't store for very long of course, and if it hadn't been used within a certain amount of time, the blood was used as fertiliser on tomato plants! We have come a long way since those early transfusions - I find the progress fascinating.

Another thing - everyone who was able to, had to get out of bed when the air-raid sirens went. Formerly, patients who had hernias or appendix and so on, had to lie up in bed for fourteen days. We discovered that when they had to get up during the air raids, carrying their tubes and bits and pieces about with them, that they were perfectly alright, and on the mend that much quicker. Lying in bed all that time hadn't been necessary. That was another step forward.

When Lord Louis Mountbatten arrived in Rangoon, he had a tremendous effect on morale. I think that the Mountbattens were a thing apart. Lady Edwina certainly did her duty, and came to the hospital in her Red Cross capacity. Lord Louis had this tremendous presence. He came to the hospital as well, and whenever you saw him, he had the effect of making you feel that all was well. He had a sense of humour too, and he used to say, "I know I'm good-looking, but I can't help it!"

Lord Louis and General Slim both had this great charisma, which worked wherever they went. Monty had the same effect in the Middle East.

They have said all these bad things about Mountbatten since, and that makes me very cross. He did a terrific job in Rangoon. Churchill has had the same treatment: "The evil that men do lives after them." - and all of that. It is quite wrong.

So we prepared the hospital; we put up three thousand beds. Then the big thing - the POWs from the Jap camps started to come in. Before that experience, you had done your duty and you had cared for your patients. But it wasn't until those POWs started to come in that you really felt an emotional response. This was something different. It was quite frightful, the mental distress. You could just figure that quite a few of them would never be the same again. Some of them were stark, raving mad. Some of those fellows had just preceded us on ships to Singapore, and hadn't even lifted a gun before being taken prisoner, and they had that grievance.

There were two doctors from the RVI among the prisoners, and they couldn't get over the equipment we had in the hospital. They had been struggling along in the most desperate conditions for three years in prison camp, doing the best they could, making needles out of bamboo and that kind of thing.

When the POWs came, the medical staff were put on half rations. I can also remember that they showed the POWs pictures of Belsen; the idea being that this would help them to realise that they had not been alone in their awful plight.

Even today there is a feeling that those people who fought and worked in Burma have been missed out, because they were so far away. There was far more emphasis on the war in Europe and the Middle East. Even Lord Louis said that we were the forgotten army. When I start to think about it, what we were fighting out in the Far East was Evil.

We had the Japanese POWs to nurse and they were put inside cages, as much for their own protection as anything else. It was complete dishonour for a Jap to be taken prisoner. I have always said that it didn't matter what nationality you had to nurse, you treated them all properly. But when I attended the Jap prisoners on night duty, I used to go into the cages accompanied by two orderlies, because the Japs were so angry at the position they found themselves in, that they used to fight and spit.

I am afraid that I still do feel uneasy about the Japanese. Although it's silly, there are certain things I won't do, like buying a Japanese car.

We had our hands full in Rangoon, but even so, we had a bit of time for recreation. Rangoon was terribly humid and we felt very sluggish, so the Colonel suggested that we took up a game to wake our systems up, shake up our livers...So we took up hockey, which is India's national game, and if you've ever seen an Indian playing hockey....I got my nose broken! I had come all the way through the war intact until then.

When I was out in India, British rule was coming to an end, but it was still a great thing to be British there. I had a love/hate relationship with India, but I wouldn't want to go back there now that the days of the British Raj are passed. There was law and order under the British.

When I came home from the war, I thought at the time that I'd never seen anything quite so beautiful as England.

## CANON PRITCHARD M.C.

The Church has always accompanied armies to war, in recent times in the shape of the Chaplain's department. Chaplains are commissioned officers in the army and airforce, though not in the Royal Navy. Canon Pritchard served in France and North Africa and was awarded the M.C. for his role in extracting the wounded from the battlefield of El Alamein. Montgomery once said that his chaplains were more valuable to him than his artillery. Canon Pritchard, at one point dubbed 'The Vicar of Tobruk' was one of those chaplains. God is but rarely mentioned in other accounts of war included in this book. Canon Pritchard redresses the balance with an account entirely dominated by his unshakeable faith in God, and his propensity to find religious symbolism in events, at the evacuation from Dunkirk for example.

# CANON PRITCHARD M.C.

I like to be prepared for things. For a long time, since quite early on in the thirties, I had felt it in my bones that there was going to be a war. It was instinctive. But I think that any intelligent person at that time would have realised that war was likely. It wasn't just Hitler. It was the whole German nation. They were hell-bent on war. There they were in 1938 in Czechoslovakia, the next year in Poland, killing people. Who did they think they were?

At university I joined the Officer Training Corps. In 1937, I got my commission and in the same year, there was a vacancy in the Chaplain's Department for this part of Northumberland, and I volunteered. My church at that time was Merton St Mary's at Dalton Le Dale in County Durham. It had been the Chapel of Ease for the monks at Durham Cathedral and during the summer they went there, to this lovely spinney which went from the main road down to the sea. Then came the blithering collieries and sunk a shaft there and it became a mining village, and everything was tarnished with it.

I preached at Hexham Abbey on St George's Day in April 1939, a day that is observed as a very special one by soldiers in Northumberland. For three centuries almost, the Northumberland Fusiliers have served under the emblem of the garter - St George slaying the dragon of evil. That morning in 1939 I said in my sermon that people would almost certainly be required to fight against tyranny, against the evil that in deed turned out to be darker than normal minds could imagine, let alone foresee. I took as my theme the story of the Men of Merrows who did nothing as their land was invaded,. and only came out to share in the victory which they had done nothing to win: "Curse Ye Merrows. Curse Ye bitterly the inhabitants thereof,for they came not to the help of the Mighty."

Some people thought that there wouldn't be a war; that we would get away with it. The majority of people did not want a war and were not prepared for it. If you want to know the truth of it, we were caught with our pants down. It was terrible; there was nothing like enough equipment to start with. When we were training, men were using broom sticks over their shoulders in drill because there were not enough rifles. It was real Dad's Army stuff. That was all true! The government tried to save money by not making armaments - but of course they had to make them in the end. The Germans caught us on the hop really. There's no doubt that that's why Hitler got away with so much. Chamberlain saved us a year in preparation, but that's all he did.

I was called to the Colours forty eight hours after the declaration of war. Boom! Boom! There was no time to do anything then. When I look back on it - Gosh Above° And we were expecting our first baby too. But my wife is a wonderful woman. She is so placid. Anything that comes, she is the most placid person you could ever meet; an exception. I am not placid.

Then there was a period of preparation, of training; courses on first aid, dealing with poisonous gasses - all kinds of things which I forget now.

The next thing that stands out in my mind is the retreat from Dunkirk. As we were retreating, the lorries and cars and trucks were piling up - there were so many that everything just came to a dead stop. I have never seen a traffic jam like it. All the chaps were milling around the trucks. We had to immobilise our vehicles so that the Germans couldn't use them. I had upended my little Ford, then used a pick-axe to knock it to bits. So I had to carry all my stuff, including my communion case, the most important thing for a padre. I had to lug that with me all over the place.

People had left their houses, left them open, run away. But there were all these soldiers everywhere and I said, "I'm going to hold a service in one of these empty houses for anyone who would like to come." And do you know, quite a few came. We had our service against this background of gunfire, bombs and all this noise and commotion; a service in the midst of it all.

Then we went down to the beach, and there were all the chaps marching into the receding sea. But the sea there is phosphorescent, you know, and as the soldiers waded through, they splashed sparkles of light as they proceeded along. "Lighten our darkness, we beseech Thee Oh Lord." I knew that God was in the midst of things. He hadn't left us. We were in God's hands.

I would like to think that this is what I brought to the soldiers at that time. I have never doubted God's reality for a moment. These experiences that come along only go to confirm what you already know.

I followed the soldiers into the sea. I can remember holding the doctor's bag high up above my head, as I stood up to my shoulders in water. I was a big chap, and he was a small one and he couldn't get to a boat without getting his bag soaked. In the end, we got away safely.

I became attached to the Royal Sussex Regiment who greeted me as one of their own. The Colonel of the regiment was the most marvelous man - Sir William Whistler the painter - a most magnificent man.

I was sent out to the Eighth Army in the desert. The War Office seemed to say, "Well, here's a north country fellow. How far south can we send him?"

I was at the Battle of Alamein. The battalion that I was with got knocked to bits. Out of our four hundred men, only sixty four were left. The majority were taken prisoner. The chaplain always works closely with the doctor, and at dusk I found myself with an ambulance and some of the wounded - everyone else had gone out of line. When I looked into the distance, all I could see where the Germans getting ready to train on us. I thought "My Goodness to me - I've got to get everyone out of here." I had to take command. So I said "Come on chaps. We've got to get out of here." (Canon Pritchard won an M.C. for his initiative and bravery.)

I knew that the track we needed to get out was called Hat Track. We managed to get so far with the ambulance and whatever transport we had. I led them along the main track and after a bit, we caught up with a chappy, and I asked him the way to Hat track. Well, he answered with such a burst of swear words, of which I had never heard the like before. But in the end, he told us the way.

But do you know, the self-same man looked me up and came to visit me in 1988, and he wrote in our visitors' book, "Last met at 0.300 hours at Alamein 1942." It's extraordinary you know, you go

133

along in the world and you don't think that anybody has taken any notice of you, but that chap remembered and came to see me all these years later.

Churchill made the observation that before Alamein we never won a victory and that after Alamein, we never lost one. The place, Alamein, was originally the dwelling place of one of the early desert fathers, St Menas, a persecuted christian Greek, who had retreated there to live in prayer and solitude. After the battle, the Greek Orthodox Archbishop issued a card on which he said that the Greeks shared with us in our victory, because he was sure that the saints had been on our side.

After Alamein, I was in Cyrenacia, at a place where we had a hospital for the wounded. My first job was to put up the Church tent and to equip it. I didn't have a cross, so I asked one of the Royal Engineers if he could make one. After a month, he produced a beautiful cross. The wood came from an Italian gun carriage, and the brass from a German anti-aircraft shell. Look —he didn't know what he was doing, but he had made the plinth for the cross as three steps: Father, Son and Holy Spirit. And the brass cross was screwed on to the wood with five brass screws —the five wounds of Christ. And the name of the Royal Engineer who made the cross turned out to be - Love.

After Alamein, the central supply point for advancing troops going west , to meet up with American troops coming from the east, was Tobruk. While we were there, I opened a Wayfarers centre , for travellers on the way, where they could meet and talk for an hour or so, and drink a cup of tea or coffee. I think it was because of that, that I was dubbed the 'Vicar of Tobruk'.

I have always been fond of the word 'vicar'. I have always enjoyed being called vicar, thinking of the vicarious suffering of Our Lord - how he suffered for others. A vicar is here to follow his example. The first sermon I ever preached was "I am among you that serveth." and I have tried to live up to that all my life, and to get that message accross to people, rather than "I am among you as he that can grab everything he can get."

MRS IRENE SALMON.

What may seem like small steps can mean big changes in a person's life. Irene Salmon had joined the ATS before the outbreak of war, and reported for duty at North Shields Drill Hall on September 3rd 1939. Her war service never took her away from the North East but even a posting to Stockton on Tees can be seen in a new light when, as she comments, most of the ATS recruits who were driven off with her that September day, "had never been away from North Shields before." The lives of many people in the 'thirties were indeed closely bound to home and locality and the war had an effect in increasing geographic mobility. The divide between the armed forces and the Home Front blurs in a war like Mrs Salmon's: never that far from home (though it would seem a long way), but subject to military discipline; she experienced air-raids on North Shields,and enjoyed military two-steps at dances in Stockton. She looks back with some affection on her service in the ATS in which she progressed from orderly to clerical duties and had some good times. It made her more outgoing, she concluded, and one feels that it did the same for many others.

MRS IRENE SALMON.

When my friend and I joined the ATS , it was just like a weekly
social club, in the Drill Hall at North Shields. It was just to
fill in a night really, that we joined. I led a very quiet life,
working as a nursemaid in North Shields, coming home for my tea
every evening, and then settling down to my knitting. My mother
used to say "Why don't you get yourself out more. Go to the
pictures or something." but I was very reserved at that time.

When I first joined the ATS, we didn't have any uniform . We were
taught how to march and salute and call the officer Ma'am. When
war was declared there was a mad rush to get kitted out. It
was hilarious - my hat was too big, my skirt was too long and
they'd run out of shoes so I had to wear Wellingtons. Oh Dear!

The evening of September 3rd 1939, I had to be at the Drill Hall
by 6pm. This great big army truck took us away and all our
mothers were there to see us off. We were all about eighteen or
nineteen and most of us had never been away from North Shields
before. All our mothers were there to see us off, and they were
crying. But we were back home the next night. They only took us
as far as Walker, so I could travel to work and back by bus.

I wasn't qualified for anything, so I was just an orderly. My
first job was just cutting endless slices of bread and making
sandwiches for the soldiers.They were Ack Ack men on the guns.

I remember one lovely sunny day after lunch, my friend and I
wandered accross the fields to sunbathe. We knew that if the air
raid siren went we had to go back and get into a big dugout
they'd made for shelter. Well, we were quite far away and as we
were lying on our backs chatting, these big clods of earth
started landing on the grass round us. We looked round and we saw
these soldiers were hurling these clods at us to try and get our
attention. We jumped up and started running like mad. There was
an air raid warning on. One of the soldiers yelled, "Get your
bloody heads down!" It was terrifying at the time but one of the
things that you laugh about later.

Then we transferred to a big house on the corner of Leazes
Terrace in Newcastle, and my job as an orderly was just to clean
the billets. I had to make out the laundry lists and I have got

tidy handwriting, and one day this officer said to me, "What are you doing in this job if you can write like that?" The next day I was sent to another post. They promoted me to writing and filing the soldiers' records, and working on the switchboard. It was much more interesting, although all the important messages came through in code, bypassing the switchboard, on a direct line to the Major.

I went to different offices all over Northumberland and Durham. But the bad thing about my better job was it meant that I was billeted away from home and Oh Dear, I was homesick. I cried every night for about six months. It was such a big change you know. In fact, I ran away once. I was on weekend leave and I didn't go back. But the military police came to collect me. The officer wasn't all that nice to me and I was confined to barracks for a time. But it was all so vastly different from the quiet home life that I had been used to; an entirely different life style.

At my first billet, three of us had to share a double bed, and that was a bit of a scramble. At Heaton, we slept in Nissen huts with the beds in a row down either side. Then we moved to a big old fashioned house, with three to a bedroom. Friday night was Barrack night and you had to stay in and clean your bedroom, have a bath and a medical inspection for any rashes or diseases.

Our first uniforms had been terrible, but they improved. We were measured for them, they were in very smart gabardine. We two of everything and Eeh, the knickers were made of Khaki silk. Then we were issued with blue and white striped pyjamas and when we first got them, on Barrack night, we all changed into them and did a conga all round the house. The leader of the conga was going to take us out the front door, but the officer stopped her. We did have some good times. They were strict with us , but we had plenty of laughs.

The food was good and there was ample . If you wanted seconds, you got seconds. We never went short. My friend and I made it first priority to make friends with the cook of any camp we were in. You could often go and get sandwiches in between meal times from them. When you were on leave, you always got a ration card and ration allowance. It's always easier to cook for a few people, than for one. I live on my own now and it costs me as much to feed myself and my dog as it does for my daughter to cater for her family.

Another job I had, at Boldon, was working on the petrol and oil accounts. You had to keep a written record of every single vehicle that came in and do the accounts at the end of the week. I had to keep records of all the vehicle repairs and get all the different technical terms right.

We went to the odd dance. We had a Fancy Dress Dance when I was at Stockton. When I was young, I had bright, ginger curly hair and I went as a Haiwaian in a grass skirt, after steeping myself in a bath full of crystals which stained your skin brown. We danced the military two step, the Palais Glide and the old fashioned walz, and fox trots - some modern dances too. I didn't know all the dances but once you got the rhythm in your head, you could fit all your steps to the music. If you've got a good partner, you don't really need to be taught.

We put on a concert once. The ATS wore their uniforms back to front and wore masks and the effect was hilarious. On the night of the concert we were jumping about the stage, and I managed to fall backwards over the footlights. I hurt my back and ended up in hospital for five months, in the RVI. Then I went home and my back still wasn't right and my mother wanted to keep me there and look after me. But this wasn't allowed. They sent a military ambulance for me to take me back to a military doctor, not my own doctor, for treatment. They said I wasn't a civilian, I was military, so that was what I had to do.

We were much luckier than in some places, but there were quite a few air raids round Newcastle just the same. Once I was on leave, going on the bus from Cullercoats to North Shields, when I noticed police, and crowds, in Stephenson Street. I got off the bus to see what was going on. The Wilkinson's Factory had been hit and the factory floor and all the machines, had caved in on the air raid shelter in the cellar beneath. When I got there, they were bringing out the bodies, and bits of bodies in plastic bags. I felt physically sick. I cried all the way home.

We had a garden shelter, which was called an Anderson shelter,at home. It was very cramped and not at all substantial. One week when I was on leave and so was my father, the siren went every night at 11pm. My father wouldn't go in the shelter, but paraded up and down the street in his tin hat. You listened for the planes and you knew the German ones, because they had a different throb. This night, you could hear the bombs whistling down, they were so close. My father suddenly appeared in the shelter, giving us a start, and he said "Ee Bugger, that was close." and the Rex Cimema two streets away had just been hit.

We travelled back from leave on the train and we had to be in by 11pm. We were always warned about being late, and we used to say the train had been held up.There were always searchlights over the train, but this one night, the train stopped and all the lights were doused. We sat shivering, listening to the bombs. Although we got a document signed at the station to prove the train had stopped, the officer in charge wouldn't believe us until the facts were checked.

Most of the officers were alright, some were very nice. That officer was a tough one - Toffee Nose, we called her. She was a right Madam. Another one I didn't like at all was a titled one from Scotland. She was a stinker. She definitely looked down on you and talked down to you. Who she thought she was I don't know. She had one of the highest ranks going and I don't think she'd seen anything of the war.

By far the worst officers were those who had been promoted from other ranks.It went to their heads. I was offered the chance of promotion but I didn't take it. I was very happy where I was, with my friends. Once you were promoted, you weren't supposed to mix. A private couldn't mix with a sergeant when they were wearing uniform, but they could when they were in civies. It was ridiculous.

Half way through the war, I met a Fusilier who I married. We were only able to get together on leave. We never lived together, had a home together. You met a lot of people in the war, and he was away and he met another woman. I don't know if he meant anything by it, but I wouldn't have it and I didn't want any more to do with him. We were divorced later, but I was discharged in 1944 because I was expecting my first baby.

My time in the ATS made me a lot more outgoing. The only real disappointment for me was that as I had been discharged, I couldn't go to the Victory Parades in London. I was very sad about that. I would have loved to have been there.

The military training in the ATS had another lasting effect on me. I still feel inclined to march. I do a lot of walking because it saves money when you are on a pension, but I also enjoy it. If there's nobody around when I'm out, I find myself swinging along the pavement.

LOUIS   SWALLOW.

From necessity, British Agriculture expanded greatly during the
Napoleonic Wars and World War 1 and then again during World War
11. Louis Swallow had been brought up in the years between the
wars, a time of severe agricultural depression, which affected
both his own family - he was one of thirteen children and his
father was a tenant farmer - and his outlook. At the outbreak of
war, he was working on a farm near Hexham. Farming was naturally a
protected occupation and he had no desire to be a soldier. To
farm well was what war-time government required of him, and what
he required of himself. The war impinged little on his way of
life although he did his Home Guard stint without interest but
with good grace.

LOUIS SWALLOW.

I was eighteen when war broke out, and I worked at Foggat Farm in
the Shire, just near Hexham. When I first went to work, I had to
stand in Hexham Mart to get hired, at nine shillings a week.
There were two hiring days a year when you could do that; 11th
November and then 13th May. Those were the same dates when you
could take your holiday; a week from the 11th November, before
they got the beasts in for the winter, and a week from May 13th.
That was all the time off you got. You didn't really get days off
- you worked the week round. If the farmer's wife was a nice
person and looked after you reasonably well, then that was worth
another shilling or so a week to you.

The thirties had been a very hard time for farmers and my family
had left the farm which they rented, Newbiggen Hill, near Hexham.
Some pulled through and some didn't, but even all these years
later I am still annoyed with my family because I saw no reason
why they shouldn't have pulled through. They had thirteen
children, and some of us could have worked on the farm - it would
have made sense, because the families of farmers were only paid a
few shillings a week in those days. So I had to start from
nothing - I am not the only one who has gone through this of
course - but it has taken my wife and I all these years to get to
the position that we are in now.

The day that war broke out doesn't stand out in my mind. The
farmer I worked for at Foggat Farm had a tractor and did contract
work, and I looked after the farm. That Sunday was just the same
as usual.

I have never been a fighting type of person, a soldier type of
person. Farm workers were needed in the war and they weren't
called up until they were twenty five, so I was able to just
carry on working on the farm. My mate down the road wanted to
join up, but they sent him back. "We've got plenty of men. You go
back and grow some food." That's what he was told.

I was conscripted into the Home Guard, but I didn't go much. The
times that I had to go, I went. And whenever I went, I was picked
to come out and march and parade in front of the rest. I don't
know why they didn't pick on one of the sergeants or someone like

that. Yes - at the time, I liked to think that it was because I was a good example!

One day a fighter plane came down in the field near the farm, and I had to dash in and get on my Home Guard's rig-out, and get there as fast as I could. By the time I got there, the pilot was having a cup of tea in a house nearby. Of course, they were all a bit worried about it; they had to make sure he was British first. We went up to the field where he'd come down and we saw that he had just missed this fence with barbed wire running accross the top, and part of the parachute was on it. He had just missed it - he could have torn his leg off...or his head...his aeroplane had come down in a ball of fire.

There weren't that many bombs dropped on Northumberland, but I can remember three craters on the Hexham/Allendale Road, from three small bombs. Another bomb was dropped at High Oustey, and it was reckoned that some car lights, or house lights, had been left on instead of being blacked out. Various stories went around.

A Lanacaster bomber came down at Knock Shield between Allendale and Allendheads. It had dropped on this poor bit of fell, very boggy land. It's big engine was nose down in this bog, oil everywhere on the surface. They left it there. I don't know if it has ever been moved. Another time, a huge, black, German bomber flew over, going East. Where it came from, we never knew, but it was pursued by two Spitfires and all the way they crisscrossed him and they were obviously just waiting to get him once they got out to sea. He couldn't do a thing about it, he was too big and too slow.

One of my brothers was a rear gunner in the airforce; he was three years older than me. He was killed. To be truthful, we weren't very near. He was quite rough on me when we were growing up - pummelled me around quite a bit. I was the small boy, the young one, and I got the feeling that they wanted to keep me that way, keep me down. But never mind, you get over these things. It takes all kinds to make the world and that's about the size of it.

Like most farmers in the war, we were fairly lucky for food; we took no hurt for milk or eggs and we ate a lot of pork and bacon, everybody roundabout kept their own pig. We had any vegetables we could grow. You grew fields of turnips to feed the animals. You hadn't the hay for hay feeds, and the animals had to eat the straw from the grain, the corn stalks, so the cows didn't produce such a great amount of milk. You couldn't get so much off the land before the modern fertilisers. You used manure from the farm mainly, and you'd be lucky to produce two tons of crops from an acre, whereas now you can get three tons.

If you wanted entertainment, you went to whist drives or dances. To get to a dance at Whitley Chapel, I only had to bike three miles. When I started courting my wife, who I met in about '42, I had to ride ten or twelve miles up to Keenley and then back again.

I didn't drink and I didn't smoke much, so I was able to save, and by the end of the war or thereabouts, when I was earning two pounds a week, I had saved about seven hundred pounds. I had all my board and lodging included with the job, of course. We didn't marry until six years after we had met, because we didn't have the money, or a farm to take on until then.

I've always been in dairy farming. During the war, we had a milking machine at Foggat Farm, which was alright if you could get it to start up. Quite often, we had handmilked all the cows before it would get going, because we had to be ready on the dot for the milk cart coming to collect the milk for the dairy. I remember a farmer telling me in about 1940, that if a dairy farmer had made one hundred pounds' profit, then he had had a good year.

We didn't have to start work too early, about 6.30 or 7 a.m. Then you finished at about 6 p.m. The hardest days were the threshing days, leading corn in, because you had a long carry with these heavy sacks and you had to hump them up the steps to the loft where they were stored.

It was just day to day life for me during the war. I did my bit for the Home Guard, but as soon as my duty was over, I forgot all about it, put it right out of my mind, and was back thinking about my cows and the farm there. I mean a farmer is a farmer. People in different walks of life have different ideas, but I think that for most farmers, they've got their love for their land and their love for their animals, and that's that.

ANDREW WOODCOCK.

There was conscription in 1939, but Andrew Woodcock, although he was in a protected occupation, was already a territorial in the Northumberland Fusiliers . That his enthusiasm for the army and for his country was dispelled, is understandable when one considers that for the most part, his war-time experiences were those of defeat. Dunkirk was after all a defeat, even if silver linings could be found in the fact that so many troops were successfully evacuated, and much blame can be put upon the debacle of the French army. Singapore was the nadir of the British military tradition, and Andrew Woodcock and his fellow Fusiliers arrived there just in time to be captured by the Japanese. After that, it was work on the Burma railway, illtreatment by the Japanese, the amputation of an ulcerated leg and semi-starvation. His eventual release with the Allied victory was marred by further blunders and crass insensitivity; the army couldn't even organise his return to Newcastle properly.His experiences were particularly unfortunate and one can sympathise with his view of things. His account bears out the feeling shared by others who fought in the Far East, that they were "the forgotten army".

ANDREW WOODCOCK.

I was a pitman, and as miners were exempt, I didn't need to join
up, but all me mates joined the territorials, so I did too. It
was the comradeship that I enjoyed.

By the time that war broke out, there were so many territorials
in the Northumberland Fusiliers, that they formed two more
battalions. One of them was my battalion, the 9th Battalion. The
original 9th Battalion had been wiped out in World War 1, and
reforming it was, for us, the worst thing they could have done.
Because of its history, we classed the 9th as a jinxed battalion.

We went over to France in 1940 and we were there for seven weeks.
I was driver to the company commander, Captain Wilkinson. He was
a smashing chap. When the blues started (i.e. when the Germans
attacked) I drove him round in this 1500 weight truck. He would
get the map out and show me where we were, where the Germans
were, and he would say, "You've got to get X place, but how we
get there, I don't know." He would leave it to me to sort out and
then he would sit back and fall asleep! He wasn't frightened; he
wasn't that type of bloke. A lot of the officers were worse than
us for being frightened.

Before Dunkirk, Captain Wilkinson and I drove to places that a
lot of the lads didn't go to. We went to villages that were all
deserted, towns where there wasn't a soul in sight: Arras,
Bethuen, Mereville. All our guns were put out in the different
villages, and then it quickly became like everything else in the
British Army then, withdrawal, withdrawal, withdrawal.

At Dunkirk we were on the go all the time. Our battalion.was a
pioneer battalion that had never seen action before, but we went
into action with the remaining guns. We were fully trained and
one of the best battalions in Britain at that time.

At Alnwick Castle, you can see a telegram that the Brigadier sent
to us, congratulating us on stopping the Germans where we did.
That was terrific for us, because who followed us up, and fast,
but the Guards.

But Dunkirk was a shambles. The reason for that was that the army
hierarchy was in a shambles too. I am very biased against this

146

country you know. The British Army went to France for nothing, before Dunkirk. I still feel the same way now; very biased about it yet. There were other things in the war which made me feel this way, which I'll come to later.

Our next destination was the Far East. We embarked from Liverpool, went accross to Nova Scotia, where we boarded a ship which looked a bit like a huge banana. It was an American passenger ship, and it took us for a good part of our journey. We were the first troops to be transported on American ships. It was good - smashing food.

We set off in a big convoy. We had the Mount Vernon and Miss America with us too. We went to Trinidad then accross to Capetown. The ship developed a problem on the way to India, so we had to go to Mombassa, which stank in those days. From there, we went on to India and up to Deolali Camp. You know the expression 'deolali tap', a bit gone in the head. As far as we knew, there had been a cholera epidemic at Dulali and it was what you called cloud cholera, and it left you a bit funny in the head, if you survived it.

We went back to Bombay and boarded a French boat, the Felix Roussel. We had a job cleaning it up to make it fit as it had been used to transport Italian prisoners and it was filthy. I was supposed to have been promoted to Lance Corporal, and the papers where supposed to have come up while I was on the boat, but they didn't, so I was still orderly corporal.

Well, all the lads became very sick on this boat, and no one could discover what was causing it. Then they found it was rats in the water tank. But things were that bad, that they decided that if things hadn't improved within another twelve hours, we were going to turn back. Then this sickness suddenly cleared up, just like that. But if we hadn't started to recover within that time, then we would never have been part of the Fall of Singapore. That is what I mean about a jinxed battalion.

We got to Singapore on 7th February. As we came in the RAF were bombing and Singapore was burning. Three Jap planes were shot down from our ship, but we were hit and three of the lads were killed, but we weren't sunk. The Empress of India, which was behind us, was hit and sunk.

147

It was Dunkirk in reverse - we came out of Dunkirk with the burning and the smoke and the destruction behind us. We came into Singapore with all that infront of us.

We landed, and the Battalion separated out. It is well known that the British operation in Singapore was a disaster, and that is another reason I feel so biased. We were supposed to go into concrete gun positions, but the first thing we were told was, "You have got to dig your own positions." And we could see the Japs from where we were. The digging had to be done at night, and we had a platoon of Indians on with that. There were any amount of army vehicles, but they gave me some old Chinese one and I was running the platoon around, and cooking for sixteen of us.

It was just action then, when the Japs landed. We had arrived in Singapore on 7th and it was all over by 15th. It was the civilians who were getting killed. The bombers came over in a V formation; you heard machine gun fire, then they dropped the bombs. That was the first we ever heard of 'pattern bombing'.The whole lot would come down and afterwards, the biggest stone would have been reduced to a small pebble.

When our troops, including the Argyll and Sutherland Highlanders, 880 men one month earlier, now down to ninety, had came out of Malaya at the end of January, they blew the causeway once they got into Singapore. Singapore is only a small island and there was only one water supply, and that was now full of dead bodies, so there was no water.

The stories we heard from the Aussies and the Indians were that the withdrawl from Malaya had been a real panic station, a disgrace the way it was handled. A lot of the lads felt that, and still do to this day.

We were taken to Changi Prison. We were formed into working parties from a place called River Valley Camp. The first job we had was to clean up the Alexandra Hospital, ready to receive the wounded Japs from Burma. We didn't know to the full story of what had happened at this hospital: which was that when the Japs arrived, the RAMC officer had greeted them with a white flag in the hope of protecting his patients. The opposite happened. All the RAMC officers were bayoneted to death, then the Japs ran wild through the hospital bayoneting all the patients. When we got there, you could see all the marks and signs of this rampage but all the bodies had been taken and buried. We had to clean the hospital up.

Any food supplies that had been brought into Singapore before it fell had been left sitting in the docks. Some food had been brought up to the hospital for the Jap wounded, including some big Canadian salmon in a box. Well, we were the biggest scroungers out. We were the biggest thieves! We stole one of the salmon, and the Malay who worked in the cookhouse saw us and reported us to the Jap cook. There were six of us involved, and when the Jap cook came out, we thought "We're going to get a right beating here." which is what normally happened. They beat their own soldiers when they did wrong or failed to carry out orders properly. But this Japanese was a Christian, and he said, "You English Christians no good! You steal everything." And he let us off, but mind, we didn't have our salmon.

You met these different types in prison, and some of the guards were very rough and hard, but some were alright.

Then from Changi Camp, we had the long march into Thailand. When they told us we were going, I had to decide whether to wait for my mate who had gone down with diptheria,and go in the last party to leave – or whether to go in the party I was in, with the lads. I didn't know what to do. I tried to go and see him to discuss it, but the Sikh guard wouldn't let me in. The Sikhs could be worse than the Japs.

So we set of on this terrible march through the jungle to Thailand. It took about four days. I'd lost all my equipment in Singapore, I hadn't even a blanket. It was that hot, it was a mercy I didn't have anything to carry. Other lads were just chucking things off their load. The officers were doing it too. You could just pick up anything you needed.

We got into Thailand and there was a main base camp, but you were all put into different groups. I was lucky, I was put into what was called the Hundred Camp (one hundred men). Then we were set to work digging embankments for the Thailand/Burma railway. All you had to do it with were shovels made from old oil tins, and they used to bend as you stuck them into the ground.

Then there was blasting through the cuttings with dynamite. The Jap guard used to be standing out on the road, furthest from the explosion. They didn't use long fuses, only short ones, and the chap nearest to the blast had to run like Hell.

We worked on the Bridge over the River Kwai. That film they made about it was disgusting; it was nothing like that. It romanticised the whole thing. There weren't any fellows with cotton shirts on. All we had were loin cloths. The film made it look like a holiday resort. They've made another one."The return of the River Kwai and that will probably be a load of lies and all.

The conditions of work were terrible. You had to build an embankment twenty foot high and you had a certain metreage to do every day, and you were kept there until you'd done it. You got slapped on the back with a bamboo cane otherwise. The beatings were terrible if you got in with a bad lot of Japs.

I was lucky because I also worked in the Jap cookhouse on the camp. The camp rations were mainly one pint pot of rice per person per day, but sometimes it was only half full; then a bit of paltry pumpkin stew which was mainly water. Sometimes you got a drop of tea. But the main diet was rice, always rice.

Working in the cookhouse, I was able to build up my reserves, which helped me to get through. We raided the Jap rations. We fed as well as them: a little bit meat, chicken, eggs. They left the cooks alone. I looked like Tarzan in a loincloth - black from the cookhouse fires.

I was lucky there, but then I was sent to the most hated camp in the whole of Thailand, which was run by a six foot three Korean - Modigama I think his name was. When you grouped up for your working party every morning, the last man in usually got a beating up, a licking. When I was there, this Modigama came along the line one day, and I was second in, but he pulled us out and gave us a beating up. Then I was stood in the river for eight hours - half of me was freezing cold and the other half was boiling hot.

Depending on the whim of the Japanese, you were moved to different camps. I was only at Modigama's camp for about two weeks. After that, we moved back up river, but I had to come down to base camp as I had caught my leg on a bamboo and it turned sceptic and this ulcer started to blow up. I was moved to where they brought some of the sick.

Around this time, what they called the Speedo started. Until then, you had worked from dawn to dusk. When the Speedo started, you were working in the dark as well.They were desperate to finish the railway. This was when it was really rough. I wasn't on the Speedo; I had been laid up with my ulcer before it started. But when the railway was finished and they brought all the sick down, I can't describe to you what the ulcer wards in the camp were like.

Lads were lying there with ulcers the size of soup plates. They had no medicines, but if you were lucky, you were sometimes given an antisceptic wash in something called papamang crystals. It was alright if you were the first to be treated, but otherwise you might be washed in the same water that had treated maybe twenty other men. But it didn't do any good like, because what we really needed were vitamins. You had nothing in your body to fight with.

There were big dystentry wards as well, and malaria wards, and the loony bin for the lads that went crackers. There were a few who had cerebral malaria and that was terrible. They had to put them in cages. There were a few who went crackers to get off work, but they definitely weren't loonies.

Ulcers increase in the heat, one day small, the next day, big. They eat into your flesh. You used to get maggots in the ulcer and the surgeon used to come round and say, "That's good. The maggots will eat all the dead flesh." Blue fly maggots - they cleaned the wound up! But house fly maggots were the killers because they eat up the good flesh, not the bad. At night you'd feel the maggots coming up to the top under your bandage, and you'd try to get them out.

In the ward, there was an Australian on one side of me and an anti-tank lad from Sunderland on the other. One of them had two ulcers and couldn't walk, and the three of us used to look after each other. One day one of us was up and the others were down, and whoever was on the up, would take care of the others.

One morning we woke up and one of them disappeared. It turned out He had started to walk home. His mind had gone. So I said, "Bring him back here and put him beside us and we'll look after him." But No. They took him down to the end of the ward , which is where they sent you if you were going to die. No more than five minutes later they came back and told us that he had died.

There was another Australian who had had his leg off; they took him outside for a few minutes air. He collapsed and died – cardiac arrest from beri-beri. There was an awful lot of that. I had most of them: dystentry, dengue fever, beri-beri. When I collapsed from beri-beri, all the lads clubbed together and managed to get me three pounds of monkey nuts. I ate the lot, till I was stuffed full of peanuts, and that seemed to beat it back.

My leg didn't improve and eventually it was just about all gone with the ulcer. The camp surgeon came round and he gave me one choice. "Do you want your leg off? Or do you want to die?" And that was it. They took you and laid you on a bamboo table with a mosquito net round it. They gave you a spinal aneasthetic, so you couldn't feel it, but you could see it. They did the amputation with a butcher's saw. They called it fork and knife surgery.

After that, I started to pick up. After you had a leg off, you got an absess on the stump, which was all the poison coming out. Once that had gone, you got the most lovely feeling in your body, a sense of freedom.

We were allowed two days' convalescence. I was known as 'Geordie'; we all were, everyone in the 9th Battalion was called Geordie. There was this big Aussie orderly who looked after us, and he says to me "Well, Geordie, I like you and I'm going to give you two eggs instead of one." Because that was what you were allowed – one egg, on your convalescence. The orderly taught me to bandage my own leg because the Japs would only spare a few men for medical duties, as they needed them on the working parties.

We were the fittest men in the camp; we played what ball games we could, on our crutches! We were called the Amputs, and sometimes worse than that, because we were the rowdiest fellows in the camp. We were getting a little bit better food by then, now that the railway was completed. The Japs had also begun to realise that they were going to lose the war, so it was in their interests to treat us better.

From my point of view, I was fortunate to have had a leg off, because a lot of lads who were roughly in one piece were sent up country to the Burma border to work. I got news that me mate, Gordon, who'd had diptheria in Singapore, was coming past in one of these working parties, F party, on his way to the Burma border.

Well, I'd become good at making cigarettes out of anything we could lay our hands on that could be smoked. We were allowed a few cents a week in Jap money, and with that, we used to get something called hag weed to smoke. We got it from the lads who used to go over the wire to get drugs and things from the Thais and the Chinese. And mind, they used to risk their lives to do this, those lads. There was one Thai who supplied us with a lot of drugs, and he was recognised by our officers after the war, for being so good. The Thais are a very happy people, but I never felt quite sure about them. I preferred the Chinese.

When I heard that Gordon was coming past, I got hold of some hag weed for him and made him some cigarettes. I went as fast as I could through the jungle compound, several miles, to get to get to the boundary which F party was expected to pass. But I was too late; I had missed them. I never got to Gordon or saw him again. He died up on the Burma border.

Before the end, when Tokyo was being bombed, they built an extra barricade round the camp and word went round that we were all going to be shot. They turned all the machine guns in towards us. But outside, the Allied troops were fighting it out in the jungle, and they weren't going to let that happen.

The atmosphere when it all ended was tremendous. The first jeep came in full of paratroopers. They got hold of the Jap quartermaster, and they took him down to Bangkok for rations. They came back loaded up high with supplies, and they stuck the quartermaster up on the top of them. He had to hang on - big, fat fellow he was - and they drove round and round the camp with the quartermaster clinging on for dear life.

We were taken to Rangoon, via Bangkok. We were put on a diet of
dehydrated vegetables, which I didn't think much of because after
three and a half years in prison, I weighed five stone.

The were about twenty Amputs in my group, and the medical officer
did everything he could to get us flown out, but no one would fly
us. So they put us on a British boat, the Empire Star, where we
were supposed to climb down steel ladders, through two hatches,
to our accomodation, which was matresses on the floor. And there
were twenty of us missing arms and legs

Our first meal on the Empire Star was a bowl of rice each. Every
single day for three and a half years, we had fed on rice. Here
we were on a British boat being given just the same. We had had
enough of it all by then. Try to picture it: there were near on
two hundred of us sitting with these plates of rice in front of
us one minute - the next minute, there were two hundred plates
full of rice being hurled out through the portholes  You've
never seen anything like it.

I am afraid that is one of things I have got against this
country. The way we were tret after all that we had been through,
really fixed me as far as this country is concerned.

After the rice episode, we all got off the Empire Star and we
refused to board it again.

We were all sitting around on the quayside, not knowing what was
going to happen next, except that we were not going on this boat.
Then this big captain with a golden beard comes along, and sees
us all sitting there. "What's the matter?" he asks. The next
thing is, he's sending messages on the wireless and he gets us on
to his boat, a troopship. That was alright. We only had two men
to a cabin, and proper food.

We came home via Suez, and by the time I got home, I had been
round the world , 34,000 miles.

When we docked in England, we were met by a thirteen hundred
weight truck, when there should have ambulances. I was put on the
train to Newcastle, and I arrived there in the dark. My mother

and sister were there, but as no one had told them anything, they were on the wrong side of the bridge. There was no one there from the regiment to meet me either, and there should have been. The way I saw it for a lot of us lads who had been out in the Far East, was that we'd been out of sight and out of mind,

After the war, I was always in work, at various different things. Now I'm retired, and as far as my leg is concerned, it grieves me that there are some things I can't do very well, like walking on the beach or in the woods, but I've never let it beat me.

WOMAN PILOT.

For some the war closed doors, taking people away from careers
that were just beginning. For others, war meant new
opportunities, wider horizons and the chance to do things that
peace-time circumstances would not have allowed. It has been
argued that both world wars led to a general change in women's
position in society and opened new avenues to many individual
women. The female pilot who gives her war-time account here,
certainly found this to be so. An adventurous person, she had
done a lot of flying in the thirties before the war took her from
a comfortable life in the country to become a commercial pilot.
Female commercial pilots had been a rarity in the pre-war world
but one eighth of this Northumbrian lady's fellow pilots in the
Air Transport Auxiliary were women.

WOMAN PILOT.

I can remember the start of both World Wars quite clearly. We
were expecting the second war. I don't think that people had been
really convinced by the Munich Agreement. Chamberlain was rather
a silly man, wasn't he?

The Sunday that war was declared, I went out to a lunch party and
I remember that it was mainly women, because all the chaps had
gone to get on with things. I can remember quite clearly the
butler coming in with his silver salver, bowing low from the
waist and making an announcement to the effect that the Germans
were already invading the country. The lady of the house was
dishing out raspberry fool, I think it was, and she paused for a
minute with the spoon in mid-air and said, "Thank you L - ."and
then sat down and continued as if nothing had happened.

There are always some advantages to these things. The war started
during the cub-hunting season, so when all the boys cleared out,
it left all these good horses for us to ride.

One of the things I had done for a bit, was flying. I joined a
flying club in the early thirties, and by the time the war
started, I had flown a variety of planes and I had been all over
the place. I could undertake a four hour flight, but planes were
quite different then, and after that length of time in the
cockpit, you were pretty stiff.

I had been in one of the teams that went over to Germany in the
thirties to the International Gliding Competitions that were held
there. So we had seen some of the Nazi activities, preparations
for war going on. There was an understanding that the sensible
thing to do with your german money was to leave it with the
Lufthansa at Cologne when you arrived, and collect it again when
you left Germany. The last time we went before the war, the guard
said, "I wouldn't take your money home; I would buy something
here and take it back with you." That made me think.

Not long after the war started, I went down to the BOAC offices
at Bristol to see what was going on. The offices they had moved
to there were nissen huts. I had no qualifications, but I was
interested in working for them, and it was better to go and see

for myself, than to send post-cards from Northumberland saying,
"Have you got a job for me?"

So I started by working in the map department. I did that for
quite a few months and enjoyed it. We were making maps for the
North Africa campaign, and redrawing the aviation maps for
Western Europe as the Germans penetrated into France. First, we
couldn't land at Paris, then we couldn't go to Tours, and after
that it was Bordeaux.

I had a lot of friends in France, and when it fell, that did cast
a gloom. Before D Day, I was based at Hamble, and I can remember
all the little boats collecting on the river to play their part
in the Invasion of Normandy.

After a time, I managed to get myself a job as a pilot in the Air
Transport Auxiliary, which was really a Ferry Pilot's
Organsiation. Our job was to fly and deliver aircraft to RAF
bases all over the place. I would have loved to have got a
commercial licence before the war, but I was short-sighted, so
they didn't pass me. But that didn't matter in wartime. You were
well paid, because you were a commercial pilot, and the women
were paid as well as the men, I think. There were about eight
hundred of us and out of that, about a hundred were women.

I was competant to fly a number of different aeroplanes -
American Twins, Wellingtons, Tiger Moths. My grade was Four-plus.
But I was very glad that I wasn't flying in the first winter of
the war. It was a very cold one, and the girls were flying back
and forth in the wretched Tiger Moths which were two-seater, open
aeroplanes.

You often shared digs with other A.T.A. girls, but no more than
three were allowed to live together in the same house because of
the risk of air-raids. I usually stayed in a pub, which I
prefered, as it was sociable and I enjoyed talking to people who
were doing different jobs from myself.

One advantage of being an A.T.A. pilot was that you never knew
when you would get home - in the early part of the war, that was,
because the system improved later. So you were let off
fire-watching duty, as you could never be certain of being there
on time.

You might have to undertake several deliveries in a day, which meant a number of journeys flying a variety of aircraft. I didn't really know about the engines. You had to get qualified ground engineers to fettle the aircraft; there were some female engineers. But I suppose I could manage to clean a carburettor.

To fly in the old days, you just had a compass and followed the line of the railway tracks. It was very nice, because you got to know the country very well, and that came in handy. I could generally look down and make a good guess at where I was, even if I didn't actually know. But there were worrying times of course. Sometimes the weather was very bad. Occasionally, you met a German or two in the sky.

It was an interesting life. When I had first joined the flying club before the war, my family used to say: "What are you doing with all this silly flying? It will never be any good to you." But you see, in the end it was good.

After I had been working with the A.T.A. for four years, I was forced to give up flying, which made me very cross at the time. It happened like this: All the A.T.A. pilots were given one of those flu jabs and unfortunately, I was one of the very few people who reacted the wrong way to that kind of immunisation. I was pretty ill. The doctor told me that not only could I not fly again, but also that there was a good chance that I might die within the next three weeks. There was absolutely nothing I could do about it. I was told that I could only fly slow aeroplanes, so I had to give up my job as a pilot, but I am still here today.

When I had recovered, I got a new job working for U.N.R.R.A., (United Nations Relief and Rehabilitation.) I spent the last year of the war skipping about all over the place. I was in Italy on V.E. Day and then in Greece on V.J. Day. We were given a day's holiday, as I remember, but as it was a day when the Virgin Mary had done something or other, it was a national holiday anyway.

Except for coming home on leave, I had been away from Northumberland exactly seven years, when I came home in 1946.

After the war, flying was different, with new rules and

regulations. You had to learn a great many more things - all
about wirelesses and so on. I think that the wireless took most
of the pleasure out of it. Before that, it was like sailing:
nobody could get at you.